CRAIG O'HARA

PANKŲ

FILOSOFIJA

O'Hara, Craig

h-02   Pankų filosofija. — K.: V. Oškinis, 1993. — 32 p.

   Knygoje pateikiama susisteminta pankų filosofinės minties ir visuomeninio judėjimo apžvalga.

UDK 316.6

i. L .969. 1993 02 18. Tiražas 1000 egz. Užsakymas 241. Leidinys 14
aidoto Oškinio leidykla. Bajninkų 4—-3, Kaunas, 3005.
ako ir spausdino Valstybinės spaustuvės „Raidė“ Kėdainių skyrius.

叛客的哲學

作者: 克雷格．歐哈拉
(Craig O'Hara)
譯者: 張釗維
(譯－系列三)

一不只是噪音

Craig O'Hara

THE
PHILOSOPHY
OF
PUNK

MORE THAN NOISE

AK PRESS

LONDON EDINBURGH SAN FRANCISCO

Copyright © 1999 by Craig O'Hara.

Layout and design by Christopher Nelson.

The Philosophy of Punk, 2nd edition
ISBN 1-873176-16-3

Library of Congress Catalog-in-Publication data:
A catalog record for this title is available from the Library of Congress.

British Library Cataloguing-in-Publication data:
A catalog record for this title is available from the British Library.

Published by:

AK Press
P.O. Box 40682
San Francisco, CA
94140-0682

AK Press
P.O. Box 12766
Edinburgh, Scotland
EH8 9YE

Cover design by John Yates.

Photograph on cover reproduced with permission, from the book
FUCK YOU HEROES by Glen E. Friedman
© Burning Flags Press - www.burningflags.com
Minor Threat at C.B.G.B's - New York City 1982
In the spirit of PUNK this permission was given in recognition of
the efforts that were made by the author & publisher in creating this
volume, but does not imply a full endorsement of the entire
contents by Glen E. Friedman or Burning Flags Press.

Back cover photograph © Karoline Collins.

Dedicated to Tony Herman
1970-1994

C O N T E N T S

On a spring day in 1998 Craig O'Hara called me up to ask if I would be interested in writing the introduction to the new edition of <u>The Philosophy of Punk</u>. I quickly said yes as I thought writing the foreword would be a pretty punk thing to do and kind of an honor. I was not sure that my writing the foreword would help sell a hell of a lot more books. It's not as if I had been in such and such a band or wrote for this or that zine but this was punk, a topic I knew quite a bit about and cared about.

By this point in my life I had known Craig O'Hara for a number of years and considered him one of my best friends on this lonely planet. Craig and I first met each other back in the late 1980s when we both attended Boston University. During those "not so glory days" Craig and I as well as a small cadre of friends went to many, many (maybe too many) punk shows up and down the east coast. Name the club, VFW hall or church basement and we probably spent some time there. In those days we saw quite a few great bands, like the underrated **Bullet Lavolta** and **Verbal Assault**, and a hell of a lot of others who were total duds. The music scene was a diverse mix of punk, hardcore, alternative and college rock.

That period was also a time of wild protest as we faced the crisis of the Gulf War. As punks it was important for us to take a serious stand on issues such as this and not get sucked in by the standard ideological arguments of the Right and the Left. This was also a period of growth in terms of how to move punk out of the musical arena and into everyday society.

Back in those days of our friendship Craig "jokingly" self-titled himself OPOC (Only Punk On Campus) and was a very quick judge of both punkers and non-punkers alike. Coming out of that Central Pennsylvania scene gave Craig a unique perspective on the over dressed and sometimes overdone urban/suburban punks and college rockers that flocked to cities like Boston.

Craig came from a much smaller scene and different time where punk was earned and not something "cool" you picked up at a convenience store as some might think today. In fact, punk was the opposite of convenient as it required effort to create and maintain any kind of sparse activity. What you had most of the time, particularly in the early days of American hardcore as many of you reading this book already know, was a house of freaks and misfits struggling to deal with each other and themselves—sometimes successfully, sometimes not.

Falling head first into the punk rock scene in 1983, Craig saw many of the great U.S. and touring European bands of record in their prime. Whether it was **DYS**, **Black Flag**, **TSOL**, **Marginal Man**, **BGK**, **Government Issue**, **Seven Seconds** or **Articles of Faith** you could find Craig in the center of the pit or working the door for a gig he set up himself. Stripped down, wild and insane, no frills punk was Craig's starting point and the path he tried to keep the music and ideals of punk moving towards. Keeping it real was a Pennsylvania tradition—just like the Amish.

Personally I have been involved in the punk rock and hardcore scene (primarily Boston and Washington, DC) for close to thirteen years now and even longer in the alternative music world if you count my early love of new wave dating back to fifth or sixth grade. I have had the opportunity to be a concert promoter, helped out in booking tours, worked in a collective, seen hundreds of bands and owned and listened to too many records. Punk has been a very good educational tool in my life and definitely been ingrained in my being.

In all of this time in the scene I have meet quite a number of characters. A number of people who cared a lot about the music, many who cared too much about the fashion, some who cared about the politics, a few who cared about the community, and some who actually and truly believed that punk was a real and viable alternative to the shit society we live in—Craig is one of the few who I have met who actually put the best aspects of these together in their daily lives.

The whole world of punk has expanded exponentially over the last decade, many would say for the better perhaps more would say for the worse. Some of the changes that have happened in the scene would never have occurred to Craig or myself but today are quite commonplace. Take the birth of vegetarianism and veganism in the punk community. Vegetarians were hippies not punks (except for **Crass**). Today vegetarianism is a staple in modern punk in quite a number of circles whether it be straight edge, hippycore environmentalists or the growing crusty punk scene. This positive phenomenon did not exist in the early to mid 1980s let alone the 1970s. Back then many punks followed the old **JFA** (Jody Foster's Army) diet of "cokes and snickers."

Another amazement is the growth of information outside of music that has occurred. Punks now seek in much greater numbers information about political topics and figures such as political prisoner Mumia Abu-Jamal and class consciousness issues. Publishers, such as AK Press can now sell books at the back of shows and get punks to read as well as simply listen to fast-paced aggressive music. This is not to say that the late 1970s and early 1980s did not have strong political leaning. One only has to look at the Rock Against Racism and Rock Against Reagan concerts to know that punk was setting itself up for some real political growth. The music today has now become a doorway to additional learning not simply an endpoint in and of itself.

Recently I had the opportunity to teach a semester long college course at Tufts University in Massachusetts on punk as a social, political, and cultural movement. To my knowledge, and to the knowledge of the dozens and dozens of punks, academics and guest lecturers I spoke with, this course was a first of its kind. The reason I decided to even take on such an endeavor was to begin to document as an academic and as a punk how the evolution of the music created a viable social and cultural movement.

Putting together this course was a grand effort.

Trying to teach or learn anything in an academic setting is a chore. The course was a balancing act of attempting to avoid creating an overtly idealist vision of what punk is while also trying to inspire my students to new heights and ideas. Dispelling some long held media misrepresentations and getting the real hidden history out was the essence of the course. It was also a great learning experience for me in terms of being reminded that punk is still a viable movement and new participants come into the movement everyday with the same hope that my peers and those before came in with. Of course everyone thinks that their time in the scene was the "salad days," but that is another debate for another day.

The major problem with trying to explain punk is that it is not something that fits neatly into a box or categories. Not surprising as punk had made the explicit aim of trying to destroy all boxes and labels. With that as a major hurdle, any project that tries to define punk or explain it must do so with very broad brush strokes. Punk and punk music cannot be pigeonholed to some spiked-haired white male wearing a leather jacket with a thousand metal spikes listening to music real loud. If that's all it was and is then I'm not even remotely interested. One of the main reasons for teaching this course was to dispel the misrepresentation of punk to students with little or no knowledge of what this scene really contains or has to offer. The stereotypes that parents, television and the media fostered had to be countered. The **Sex Pistols** may have been important to punk, but were they really worth dozens and dozens of lousy academic and pop culture music books written about them? Punk as both music and as a movement did not end with them and then pop up again some thirteen years later in Seattle as some music historians would have the general public believe. This course would be essential just to get that basic point across. But the course was about so much more than the music, which has always tended to overshadow all the other brilliant aspects of punk. For those that stay involved in the scene (and when I say involved I mean more than going to gigs and purchasing records), punk becomes something else and something more. It becomes a community and a real avenue for sharing ideas and making changes both personal and in the world.

One of the texts that I utilized to get basic conceptual information about punk across to my students was The Philosophy of Punk. Part textbook, part personal accounts, this book provides the lay person as well as the veteran of the pit with quite a bit of information on how the punk world has changed and grown over its now close to thirty year history (depending on when you date the birth of punk).

With topics ranging from feminism, gay and lesbian equality, environmental justice, violence and drug culture, communication and community and vegetarianism, The Philosophy of Punk takes a big bite out of punk and breaks it down into understandable sections for analysis. All this while not trying to lose the pure energy and fury that makes punk such a viable and thriving movement.

Now, there is the reality that no one book or one course can hope to fully capture all the insanely new, innovative and sometimes ridiculous directions that punk has taken in the States, Europe and around the world. Every time you look around these days there is a new faction popping up in the scene. We all know that if you put 100 punks in a room you'll get 100 opinions. What this book does do is give you the reader a road map to the madness. After that you make your own road.

To look back and remember when this book was first conceived and where punk was then (pre-**Nirvana**) and where it is now is to realize how badly our community needs to take archiving history seriously—because it is changing fast. I believe what Craig has done here is added a great piece of history to the punk world.

With all of the records, books, films, gigs and other material punk stuff out there we sometimes forget that our movement is a leap of faith. A belief that life matters, so don't fuck it up, and if someone else is fucking it up, do something about it. It's these intangibles that bind punks together who have never met or spoken. It's these beliefs that are expressed in our music and culture. It's these things that make us stay involved. The future of punk as a movement is in our hands. If you love the music, the beliefs or simply the raw power of punk, then grab a seat and start tearing through this fine work. Enjoy!

—Marc Bayard

Serpico, Berkeley, Ca, '93

This is the fourth printing of <u>The Philosophy of Punk</u>. The 1992 original was a 5.5 x 8.5 copy reproduced on a shitty self-serve copy machine at Mailboxes Etc. in Yocumtown, PA. Having no other means to bind them, I hand drilled two holes and slipped in binder rings. These were not meant to stand the test of time and often fell apart after the first read. The second edition was a bit more visual with the addition of multi-colored paper and full color photographs. This edition coincided with my move to San Francisco and three year employment stint at Kinko's. Though it sold well for $3-6, this method was amazingly time consuming and featured a fair amount of illegible text. Finally with an enormous overflow of mail and a desire to devote my time to other projects, I was happy to pay for a professional style printing and hand the distribution over to my new friends at AK Press. The first edition went through two printings of 3,000 copies, and this edition is 5,000. In addition to this, 1000 nicely printed copies of a Lithuanian translation have been sold with mixed response. The worst response being the Lithuanian authorities who raided the printer to stop him from distributing this "vile, rebellious, offensive document." More bizarre to me was the Chinese genius a few years back who took the time to translate and publish the text in Hong Kong.

The response to the book has, to date, been fantastic. For all the people who have written with comments, thank you. For the countless people who have written with whining complaints (a Punk tradition if there ever was one) like: "What about the internet?" "Why isn't there more on Queer Punks?" "What about good Skins?" "What about Punks in the sex industry?" "What about Punks in Mexico, Japan, Germany,...?" my response is simple. Write your own book. Put out your own record. Start your own radio show/fanzine/collective/band/infoshop/restaurant/label/distro/club...and let the world know what you think. Stop complaining.

Thanks to the following: the crazy O'Haras, Marc Bayard, Donny T. Punk and Tim Yo (RIP), Christopher Nelson, Jason Crandall, Sean Sullivan, the NWC! crew, Character Builder, Tom Brooker Band, Citizen Fish, AVAIL, Bender, Indigo Girls, Propagandhi, all of the great bands pictured, Profane Existence, FF5, OX, Pueblo CO, Holly Prochaska, anyone who bought the first edition, Michael Martin, Bernie Phillips, Ramsey, AK Press, anyone trying to do something original, positive, shocking or great.

Footnotes are written parenthetically in this manner: author or band; article, book, or record; magazine or record label date, page; and abbreviated in a readable manner when used again. For the exact source used twice in a row I have used the abbreviation "ibid." It is important not to skip over the noted sources as they often reveal extra information about the quote. A bibliography is provided at the end of the book.

In several cases neither an author nor a page number is listed. Many fanzines do not cite the authors or do not have numbered pages. I don't think that anyone can blame me for my unwillingness to count pages of a zine in order to give an exact reference. When authors are cited, they often have creative names, e.g. Jello Biafra or Kevin Seconds, or give no last names. In the case of records, there is usually a lyric booklet or information booklet enclosed from which the quote was taken. Band names are in bold and fanzine titles and book titles underlined. Record titles are followed by either "EP" (which means it is a seven inch record) or "LP" (which is a twelve inch record).

Several unfamiliar terms may be used, but all are explained throughout the book. Punkers are going to have to bear with me here; remember some of your cool parents are reading this. Very quickly, a "show" is what Punks call a concert. It is different from an average music concert because there is a goal of removing the audience/performer separation. The term is used to distinguish the two different events. The word "scene" is used quite a bit throughout the book. The "scene" is the Punk community and the word they use to describe it. There are local scenes, national scenes, and worldwide scenes. The subsections of the Punk movement also use the term to describe themselves, e.g., the Straight Edge scene. I choose not to divide the Punk scene into too many sections, but some do. For my purpose the only divisions necessary are between Punks, Straight Edge Punks and Skinheads. This is due to the visible differences in style of dress as well as differences in behavior or supposed philosophies. As I am writing this now in the San Francisco winter of '99, I could go on with describing other willingly formed sub-groups such as Riot Grrls, nerd punks, gutter punks, emo punks....

The term "Hardcore" as I use it is simply a synonym for Punk that Americans invented in the early eighties.

Hardcore music is usually faster than the Punk music of the seventies, but the ideas and people involved are virtually the same. It is important to note that I will be dealing with the ideas and not the specific musical styles (which are many). I will leave that to the music critics.

As far as I know, this is the only work of its kind. Many books have been written dealing with the movement of the late seventies, and these are all outdated and fairly irrelevant entertainment. Serious books on the Punk movement have been written on the early California scene (<u>Hardcore California</u>), the early Washington D.C. scene (<u>Banned in D.C.</u>), and the later New York scene (<u>The Making of a Scene</u>). With the exception of the classic <u>Hardcore California</u>, they are useful only for historical documentation through photographs. No books have tried to capture the philosophy of the ever changing internation-

al Punk scenes. The book Threat By Example has come closest, printing the philosophies and ideas of twenty-seven influential members of the movement. In this wonderful book the writers talk about personal experiences and influences but do not really cover many particular ideas as I have tried to do.

Between each section are collages made up of graphics and art copied from various fanzines and records. I urge the reader to look at these very carefully as they are images of the subjects I am discussing. The images do tell a story. The photographs were taken by myself and include the relevant captions. The only exceptions are the Indigo Girls photo, three or four taken by Karoline Collins, and a couple by my brother Jack. I should mention that I have been participating in the Punk scene since 1982 and believe that it is a very effective and fun way to learn about politics, how to change things (if possible), and attempt individualism and nonconformity in a way that is positive to one's own self. Punk is ever changing and the degree to which Punks are active in producing information and having agreed view points on specific issues is mercurial. I do not mean to say that the ideas I present here are the only ones (or even my own) but that they are currently the most visibly held positions of the Punk scene today.

Finally, I would like to stress that this paper was not written for just the music fan, but for the reader with interests in the political and social philosophies of others. Punks have progressed and matured in their philosophy very much from the beginnings of the movement. I do not attempt to write a history, but a documentation of a growing and changing philosophy as it looked to me on April 13, 1992, and continues to operate today. In coming years this may be completely outdated, but for my own sake and the tens of thousands of other concerned Punks in North America and Europe, I hope our scene will only change for the better.

Jim Filth, Berkeley Ca., '91

WHY PUNK:

BACKGROUND COMPARISONS WITH PREVIOUS ART MOVEMENTS; SOME DEFINING CHARACTERISTICS OF PUNK.

"In a mechanical and depersonalized world man has an indefinable sense of loss; a sense that life...has become impoverished, that men are somehow 'deracinate and disinherited,' that society and human nature alike have been atomized, and hence mutilated, above all that men have been separated from whatever might give meaning to their work and their lives." (Charles Taylor as quoted in Man Alone edited by Eric and Mary Josephson, Dell Publishing, New York, 1962, 11).

There is a current feeling in modern society of an alienation so powerful and widespread that it has become commonplace and accepted. Some trace its roots to the beginnings of the Industrial Revolution when the work place became a second home for young and old alike. It does not take a Marxist or a learned sociologist to realize the role of mass production and maximum efficiency in creating alienation. Any rivethead, phone salesperson, or warehouseman could tell us this. The peculiar part is that man has been the one who created, agreed to, and accepted these feelings as normal. Perhaps in the late 20th century we cannot remember a time without such feelings and that we are now merely inheriting the negative structures which cause alienation. Few can argue with the idea that "Western man (and Eastern as well) has become mechanized, routinized, made comfortable as an object; but in the profound sense displaced and thrown off balance as a subjective creator and power" (ibid, 10).

Human beings act as if they have nothing in common with each other. It is as if we have all been brought here to function for ourselves in a way that does not include others. Many philosophers, sociologists, and theologians have attempted to show the ridiculousness of the

Dead Boys, Enola, Pa, '86

atomistic, alienated lifestyles we have chosen. While the intellectual community has often shown the ability to see the 'big picture' of how things really are, this insight has mostly been kept to themselves in academic publications and confined to institutions of higher education. The elitism and monetary cost of the Ivory Towers insure that the number of people entering who suffer under the oppression the professors are so eager to study will remain few.

Repeatedly, however, a group of the alienated will recognize what is happening to themselves. This realization can be based on an active rejection either of or by the mainstream society. These groups can either reject the alienation they see before them or can be unwillingly alienated from the mainstream. Blacks, homosexuals, HIV+, the lower classes, etc., all have been brought together by either the realization of hierarchies or forced together by an actively destructive, authority-backed power. It is important to note that the realization of one's own group, or self, being an out-group does not entail the realization of other out-groups suffering under the same treatment. People have too often woken up to see the details of their own suffering while still remaining ignorant to the suffering of others.

Some out-groups greatly desire to be a part of the mainstream while others do not. Nevertheless, "all such out-groups face a certain degree of isolation from society; they are in the community but not of it. As a result, they tend to form more or less distinct 'subcultures' of their own" (ibid, 35). These subcultures appear to have members who are much less alienated from their own being and are often seen trying to reclaim their subjective powers. Members of subcultures, regardless of how oppressed, have often succeeded in finding a solidarity and understanding amongst themselves that is lacking in mainstream society. Members seem to regain a sense of themselves and each other that had been previously lost, forgotten, or stolen. This is seen in the emergence of support groups based on shared experiences, beliefs, sex or race. What subcultures can succeed in doing is "to imbue their members with some sense of higher purpose" (ibid, 51). This higher purpose is not always positive, as in cases such as the KKK or other hate group subcultures, but is an important component to have in any movement desiring to make changes in the status quo.

The subculture of Rock and Roll music has been an unsteady and complicated one to define. It seems idealistic and unlikely that Rock music (having started a number of years before Elvis Presley and continuing in its many forms today) has had any higher purpose than to entertain.

Rebellious youths have been drawn to its changing forms for four decades, but as a whole it has been merely another part of the ever growing entertainment industry. Early Rock and Roll vaguely addressed the racial barriers and inequalities of the fifties, but it was not until the late sixties that distinct politics were carried in Rock music. It was at this time that Rock showed its power and the subculture became a counter-culture.

A look back on the radicals of the 60's, and I don't mean the hippies who were content to wear flowers and beg for change in San Francisco, shows their passion for Rock music and the integral link Rock'n'Roll played in their politics. From the Black Panthers falling in love with Bob Dylan in Oakland, CA to White Panther John Sinclair and his **MC5** brothers calling for armed revolution in Michigan, these folks all recognized and appreciated the power of Rock music as the people's music. Prior to death and sell outs, 60's radicals Jerry Rubin and Abbie Hoffman along with countless others, channeled Rock'n'Roll to create an enormous anti-government movement made up of young dissatisfied freaks.

Unfortunately, whatever good this music served by giving praises to freedom and disdain for social hypocrisy, it met the same fate as all earlier and later forms of popular Rock: "commercial dilution/creative exhaustion, co-option and takeover by mainstream forces" (Mark Andersen, Washington Peace Letter, Nov. 1991, 1). Rock music became "either commodified, mainstream music promoted and packaged by corporate giants, or ritual, shallow hedonism" (ibid).

An exception to Rock and Roll's predictable mainstream politics and actions has been the movement called Punk Rock, or simply Punk. The time and birthplace of the Punk movement is debatable. Either the New York scene of the late sixties/early seventies or the British Punks of 1975-76 can be given the honor. For our purposes, neither one deserves a long investigation as the specific politics and genuine forming of a movement was not until the late seventies. In general it is thought that the New Yorkers invented the musical style while the British popularized the political attitude and colorful appearances. A quick look at the background of the English scene will show the circumstances in which modern Punk was born.

Tricia Henry has written a very good book which documents the beginnings of the Punk movement in New York and its subsequent rise in England. While the book is good, it ignores everything done since 1980, when she considers Punk to have died. Several books of this kind have been written (all concentrating on the largest of all Punk bands, the **Sex Pistols**) and most lack a great deal of information, as they were done by writers who were not part of the movement, but outside interpreters. Henry is, however, correct and thorough on the subject at hand.

"For the large number of people on welfare—or "the dole,"

Pete the Roadie, Washington D.C., '95

25

as it is known in Great Britain—especially young people, the outlook for bettering their lot in life seemed bleak. In this atmosphere, when the English were exposed to the seminal Punk Rock influences of the New York scene, the irony, pessimism, and amateur style of the music took on overt social and political implications, and British Punk became as self-consciously proletarian as it was aesthetic" (Tricia Henry, <u>Break All Rules!</u>, University Microfilms, Ann Arbor, Mi, 1989, p.8).

It is true that unemployment and poor social conditions provoke angry feelings of alienation and frustration. It is also true that these feelings can be expressed in many ways. Crime has been the most popular response in recent times, but at this place and time the hoodlums began playing guitars as well as committing petty crimes of frustration. "To ignore the obvious connections between the Punk

Citizen Fish, NYC, 91

phenomenon and economic and social inequalities in Great Britain would be to deny the validity of the philosophical underpinnings of the movement. Punk in Britain was essentially a movement consisting of underprivileged working-class white youths. Many of them felt their social situation deeply and used the medium of Punk to express their dissatisfaction" (ibid, 67).

The purpose of saying this is to give a basis for where the Punks are coming from and why they hold the ideas they do. It would be a lie, however, to say that these original Punks had well-developed social and political theories. They may have been against all the standard '-isms', but were more apt to spit and swear than to explain their feelings to the mainstream public. "These were Punks, not social activists, and their message was bleak. The **Sex Pistols**' music was an outburst of hatred and despair. Face life as we see it, they cried—frustrating, meaningless, and ugly. Scream it out with us...'There's no future!'" (ibid, 66).

The goal of these Punks was to express their rage in a harsh and original way. The most hated thing in the world was someone who was a willing conformist. Many Punk bands have built their platforms or messages with the advocacy and admittance of nonconformity. Conformity is rejected on every front possible in order to seek the truth or sometimes merely to shock people. What is so wrong with conformity? The noted sociologist Elliot Aronson defines conformity as the following: "a change in a person's behavior or opinions as a result of real or imagined pressure from a person or group of people" (Elliot Aronson, The Social Animal, Freeman and Company, San Francisco, 1972, 16). The real or imagined pressure that Punks reject is not only the physical kind or the interest to be accepted, but the kind of conformity "that results from the observation of others for the purpose of gaining information about **proper** behavior..." (ibid, 25).

Punks question conformity not only by looking and sounding different (which has debatable importance), but by questioning the prevailing modes of thought. Questions about things that others take for granted related to work, race, sex, and our own selves are not asked by the conformist whose ideas are determined by those around her. The nonconformist does not rely on others to determine her own reality.

The questioning of conformity involves the questioning of authority as well. Punks do not have a great deal of respect for authority of any kind, as will be noted in the section on anarchy. In general, forced authority has been looked at as a great evil causing agent. From the German Nazis in World War II, to the subjects of Stanley Milgram's shock experiments, to today's police force, it has been proven that unjustified obedience to authority has resulted in mass acceptance of harmful actions.

By acting as anti-authoritarian nonconformists, Punks are not usually treated very well by those people whose commands to conform are rejected. Our society, well practiced at doublethink and scapegoat imagery, has used language to create a negative image of those who pursue nonconformist means. "For 'individualist' or 'nonconformist,' we can substitute 'deviant;' for 'conformist we can substitute 'team player.'" (ibid, 14). This is exactly what modern society has done and its negative portrayal of the Punk movement will be seen in the section on Punk's media misrepresentation.

We have seen that nonconformists may be praised by historians or idolized in films or literature long after the fact of their nonconformity. As for their own time, the nonconformist is labeled a rebel, a deviant, or a troublemaker by the status quo she is going against. Corporate music and fashion magazines that banned or ridiculed Punk for the last twenty years now hail many bands as "ground breakers" or talented originators. Corporate music executives once disgusted by Punk are now signing young bands left and right in an effort to make money off the "cutting edge," nonconformist sounds.

Jawbreaker, SF Ca, '94

While mass acceptance may be tempting and even lucrative for some, this quote by Dick Lucas of the English bands **Subhumans** and **Citizen Fish** sums up the feelings many Punks have towards society and mainstream culture:

"I have never come to terms with the idea that I am 'part of society' and should construct my actions to suit the prevailing moods of conformity, acceptance and achievement. Closed by the rigorous mind training of school and media, the mass mentality of Western culture revolves around upholding the past to attempt to secure the future, whilst suffering the present as beyond its control, 'safe' in the hands of government who feed the present to the masses as a product of technological/material/industrial progress." (Dick Lucas, Threat By Example, edited by Martin Sprouse, Pressure Drop Press, San Francisco, 1989, 13).

Dick is not alone in his thinking. Hundreds of thousands Punk fans feel the same way. With this attitude in mind, I will attempt to show what Punk is, how it has been portrayed by the media, and some of the specifics of the philosophy.

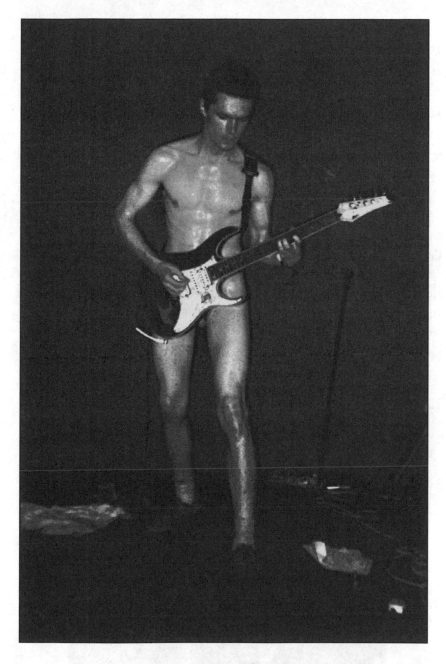

(above) Propagandhi, Nashville, Tn, '96
(below) AWOL, Harrisburg, Pa, '85

"The distinguished Soviet psychologist Pavel Semenov once observed that man satisfies his hunger for knowledge in two ways: (1) he observes his environment and tries to organize the unknown in a sensible and meaningful way (this is science); and (2) he reorganizes the known environment in order to create something new (this is art)" (Aronson, 269).

Under this definition Punk can be defined as an art form. Punk is much more than this, as it involves particular theories and politics, but when trying to understand what Punk is, comparisons to previous art movements are helpful. Early Punks (perhaps quite unknowingly) used many of the same revolutionary tactics employed by members of early avant-garde art movements: unusual fashions, the blurring of boundaries between art and everyday life,

C.O.C., Baltimore, Md, '87

juxtapositions of seemingly disparate objects and behaviors, intentional provocation of the audience, use of untrained performers, and drastic reorganization (or disorganization) of accepted performance styles and procedures.

The most frequently mentioned comparison between Punk and a known art movement is with Dada. "Dada, generally placed between 1916 and 1922, gained notoriety in France shortly after World War I for vigorously rejecting all previous existing social and aesthetic values" (Henry, 3). There have been at least three studies that I know of where Punk has been likened to a modern day version of Dada. The comparison is valid though I would guess that Punks would generally show a distaste for Dadaist art. Both are subversive but thankfully Punk appears to be less absurd and abstract about its subversiveness.

A movement to which early Punks expressed greater similarities was the Futurist movement. Futurism was a movement launched in 1909 by Filippo Marinetti with his "Foundation and Manifesto of Futurism," published in the large-circulation Paris daily, Le Figaro. "Like other movements in the historical avant-garde, it was an interdisciplinary movement which included visual art, literature and performance. It was dedicated to the rejection of traditional art forms, non-naturalist expression, and audience involvement" (Henry, 2). This audience involvement is an important link between the art and Punk movements as both have attempted to break down the standard barriers present in the performer/viewer relationship.

"As part of the Punk policy of provocation, performers were known to include in their performances behavior such as vomiting on stage, spitting at the audience, and displaying wounds that were the result of self-mutilation—having cut and bruised themselves with objects such as broken bottles, fish hooks and knives. The audiences role often included throwing 'permanently' affixed seating, beer bottles, glasses, and anything else that made itself available at the performers" (Henry, 4).

This interaction was actively pursued in the early years of Punk, but there is a very large separation becoming more apparent. As the audiences get larger and larger, concerts are becoming more entertainment than interaction oriented. Small gig halls are still hosting interactive settings but larger venues are echoing typical Rock 'n' Roll concerts. Also the performance characteristics of Punks as specified above have been extremely toned down. When these do occur, they are usually thought of as acts of unoriginal shock value or simply yearning for the "good old days" of Punk when there were no politics other than expressing rage.

Also influencing the later Punk movement was the type of dress the Futurists chose. Futurists meant to take their anti-art message to the streets by wearing outrageous clothes, earrings, and make-up. This was later duplicated by the fashion-oriented Punks of Kings Road in London.

An important difference is to remember that Punk has evolved past the 'shock tactics' of colored hair and dog collars to have a fairly cohesive philosophy with little or nothing to do with one particular style of dress. While useful at the time, and still fun today, shocking people with appearances has taken a back seat to shocking people with ideas.

These short comparisons (again, longer ones have been done) of Punk to avant-garde art movements show that Punk was not unique in its expression, or even methods, of rebellion. What needs to be done is an accurate update of what the Punk scene is and has to say in todays world.

From this point forward, I will be using sources from the Punk scene almost exclusively for information. Thousands of fanzines (magazines put out by Punks for and about Punks) have been written expressing the writers' views of what Punk is, its politics, its best music, and the writers' purpose for communication. By using these as sources I will aim to produce an accurate picture of the philosophy of modern Punk.

ABC NO RIO, NYC, '91

35

"To start with, I'll tell you what I think Punk isn't—it isn't a fashion, a certain style of dress, a passing 'phase' of knee-jerk rebellion against your parents, the latest 'cool' trend or even a particular form of style or music, really—it is an idea that guides and motivates your life. The Punk community that exists, exists to support and realize that idea through music, art, fanzines and other expressions of personal creativity. And what is this idea? Think for yourself, be yourself, don't just take what society gives you, create your own rules, live your own life." (Mark Andersen, Positive Force handout, 1985).

There have been many observers and participants in the Punk scene that have not noticed any meaningful underlying purpose. Young people are traditionally known to go through a phase of rebellion which manifests itself against parents, school, and authority in general. Punk has incorrectly been labeled as simply one of these phases in which the rebellious person tries to show that she is different from her peers. It is true that the traditional styles of dress and music of Punk Rock are often offensive and

(above) Eightball, Yocumtown, Pa, '91
(left) Ignition, Harrisburg, Pa, '88

shocking to the mainstream public, but it is misleading to think of Punk as an appearance oriented movement. Mindless, temporary rebellion can be very fun, but is not very effective or useful. Punks have evolved far enough to favor substance over style, a fact almost always ignored or twisted in media representations. It is not enough for a person to look different from the mainstream, there is an important emphasis on consciously becoming one's own self.

When people who want only to be unique or different from the rest of society adopt the Punk look, they succeed in appearing different from the norm. This is a fairly meaningless step. For someone to attempt individuality and become themselves "requires an honest, often painful look inside yourself, asking tough questions like: Who am I? What do I want from life? What should I want? What should I do? Ultimately, this process will, no doubt, make you refuse to conform to many of society's rules and expectations..." (ibid). It should be stressed that answering these questions requires further questioning of *why* do you want something, *what* are the reasons behind your desires. This process is aimed at making a person aware of himself and his own identity. In this respect the person becomes different from others. From the realization of one's own nonconformity comes the realization that society was not set up to accommodate a civilization of individuals. "Instead it is designed to accommodate some non-existent 'normal' individual and force others to fit into that mold with the end result being institutionalized dehumanization" (ibid).

Rebellion is one of the few undeniable characteristics of Punk. It is implicit in the meaning of Punk and its music and lyrics. Whether a person sticks it out long enough to learn important personal realizations or not, "everyone who gets involved in Punk is usually prompted by some form of rebellion, be it against parents, authorities, or the whole system itself" (Steve Beaumont, letter in <u>Maximum Rock N Roll</u> #53, Oct., 1987). Young people "reach the age where something clicks inside them and they feel they want to do things themselves. Kids that are fed up with conditions around them—be it socially, musically, or whatever" (Al Flipside, "What's Changed in Ten Years," Flipside #48, Feb. 1986). For those who become associated with the movement (and they need not be young people), this initial rebellion turns into a force for education and personal change.

The most important (and perhaps most radical) thing for the Punks to do is take on responsibility. This goes first for themselves and how they order and live their personal lives, then extends to include others. -What sort of responsibilities are these exactly?... "To use our mind, to treat people with respect, not to judge on outward appearances, to support others in their struggle to have the right

7Seconds, Camp Hill, Pa, '84

Underdog, Baltimore, Md '87

to 'be themselves,' even to help bring positive change to our world" (Mark Andersen).

Not all Punks agree on how to support others or bring about change outside of their own circle, but there are agreed upon necessities. As Punk is now comprised of a clear majority of middle and service class whites instead of inner city working class whites or minorities, an important action has been to reject their own privileged places in society. "We are the inheritors of the white supremacist, patriarchal, capitalist world order. A prime position as defenders of the capital of the ruling class and the overseers of the underclass has been set aside for us by our parents, our upbringing, our culture, our history, and yet we have the moral gumption to reject it. As Punks we reject our inherited race and class positions because we know they are bullshit." (Joel, columnist for the Punk-anarchist fanzine <u>Profane Existence</u> #13, Feb. 1992). If Punks were born into this world to be the sons and daughters of

America, they have instead become orphans of a fucked up society.

So what is Punk? The following three definitions of Punk must be mentioned, as they are all relevant opinions and are all true:

Punk is a youth trend. "I'll tell you what Punk is—a bunch of kids with funny haircuts talking pseudo-political bullshit and spouting liberal philosophies they know little or nothing about" (Russell Ward, letter in MRR #103, Dec. 1991).

Punk is gut rebellion and change. "Hardcore: a bleached-blonde defiant sixteen-year old living alone in a downtown hotel; sleazy but on her own. Hardcore: the S.S.I. recipient being paid off by the government to stay out of trouble and renting a rehearsal studio with his monthly check. Hardcore: the corporate flunky who quits his job to manage a band of acned adolescents" (Peter Belsito and Bob Davis, Hardcore California, Last Gasp Publishing, San Francisco, 1984, 7).

Punk is a formidable voice of opposition. "We have created our own music, our own lifestyle, our own community, and our own culture.... We are building a movement based on love, taking actions in hope that some day peace may finally be achieved. We may stumble in our efforts, but we still struggle to carry on. Freedom is something we can create every day; it is up to all of us to make it happen" (Profane Existence #4, June 1990).

While the third serves as the ideal to the other two, the first is the one most commonly presented in the media. As will be shown, this is the least accurate but the most popular image of Punk.

MEDIA MISREPRESENTATION: HOW TELEVISION, GLOSSY MAGAZINES, AND MINDLESS MASS MEDIA HAVE DONE THEIR BEST TO DEFANG THE BEAST.

"As far as most people are concerned, we're all drug crazed revolutionaries hell-bent on the destruction of all civilization. Is it a surprise then when show after show is shut down? Is it a surprise when Punks are beaten, stuffed into squad cars and taken to jail? The list of injustices is as long as the history of bad press Punk Rock has received" (Anonymous letter, **MRR** #53, Oct. '87).

Regardless of what Punk was or still is all about, it is obvious that it has received a bad reputation. Television, films, comic strips and advertising have all misrepresented Punk to the mainstream public. Punk has been characterized as a self-destructive, violence-oriented fad. During the mid-eighties, talk shows such as *Donahue* often used Punks as subject matter. Also, situation comedies such as *Alice, Silver Spoons,* and many others had episodes focusing on the embarrassment and shame involved when one of the characters "turned punk" for an episode. Of course, the character came back to his or her senses and returned to "normal" before the show ended.

In the cases of the talk shows, a member of the mainstream brainwashing groups "Parents of Punkers" or

WB·7

WB·5

⑫

33 ㉜

15 14
13

41 34 35 40 39 38 36 37

WB·9

WB·6

50 51 52
48
49 53
47

BTS·1
SPIKE BOOTSTRAP

㉕

54
72

㊵

74

SBT SID VICIOUS BELT

"Back in Control" would often be present to convince watching parents that their children could be "cured from Punk insanity" with enough money and psychotherapy. Mothers would recall horror stories about their crazy children, while an audience covered with black leather and make-up would shout and spit. How shocking to the viewing public!

Episodes of the television shows *Chips, Quincy, Square Pegs, 21 Jump Street*, and films such as *Class of 1984, Repo Man*, and many others presented Punk as a "direct cause of sadomasochism, suicide, murder, rape and other forms of violence" (Larry Zbach, MRR #22, Feb. 1985). The non-Hollywood views and attitudes of Punks will be examined in this book and shown clearly not to be the harmful stereotypes presented in these shows and films. To the mainstream ignorant viewer, however, it was and still is easy to buy "the sensational mass media images of Punks as violent, nihilist drug abusers whose main purpose in life is to wear funny clothes and dream up disturbing new hair styles—when they are not terrorizing gray haired old ladies or pan-handling money, that is!" (Mark Andersen, handout, 1985).

To be honest there have been many legitimate cases of Punk violence (usually against each other), drug abuse, and a small amount of petty crime coming out of the Punk scene. Rather than justify the media stereotype, I argue that it is precisely the media distortion that has caused the bulk of the problems.

"Repeated media distortion, exaggeration, and stereotyping help to create a type of 'punk' who has no idea of the conceptions, political and social philosophies, and diversity of the Punk movement. This type of 'punk' will join the Punk movement in increasing numbers. As they join, the media frame will literally become true. The moral authorities will be proved right and the appropriate actions which the societal control culture deems necessary to deal with the problem will be legitimized. The potential for destroying or compromising the Punk movement will be great" (Larry Zbach, MRR).

While the media image did not destroy the Punk scene, it did have a harmful effect. In large parts of North America and parts of England, portraying Punks as violent attracted people who were really violent to the scene. In these places "Punks visceral individualism and anti-authoritarianism were submerged under the weight of a sea of short-haired jocks, not to mention a smattering of petty criminals and psychopaths" (Jeff Bale, Threat By Example, 63). This was especially evident in New York City and Los Angeles where rival gangs made up of Skinheads and Hispanics were drawn to shows by the promise of the violence they saw on television.

Other "Quincy Punks" (named after the fashionable, unintelligent, violent characters portrayed on the television show) became increasingly violent towards those who did not look "punk" enough. At this time (1984-87), Punk suffered through a period of media created violence and stupidity which threatened to make Punk a parody of itself. While still saddled with its effects, the Punk scene has rejected these characteristics as the exception and not the rule.

While mainstream and conservative media touted Punk as a violent and unwelcome movement of delinquents, liberal sources were hardly better. Left wing political groups and magazines were quick to condemn Punk as a passing fad which had no real significance. The liberal press "tried to defang the beast, ignore the political and cultural cries for change, and try to do the Big Amoeba Dance; absorb an angry flurry of ferment and transform it into a nice, safe, consumable fad based on nothing more than hairdos, fashion and the revival of various musical styles" (Jonathan Formula, Hardcore California, 6).

Boston sociologists Jack Levin and Philip Lamy (then of Northeastern and Brandeis University respectively) wrote a paper in 1984 which analyzed Punk Rock. The authors dismissed the popular stereotype of violence surrounding Punks, but stopped short of acknowledging any power the movement might have. "Levin said he is confident that Punks, like other generations, will outgrow the fad and become respectable middle-class citizens as adults" (United Press International, an uncredited newspaper clipping as reproduced in MRR #19, Nov. 1984). There are quite a number of people who are now adults who could disprove the statement. These people may not have the fashionable trappings of the Punk stereotype, but possess the ideas that make Punk a movement to examine.

The dismissal of Punk as a temporary trend or fad has had an effect similar to the earlier characterization of Punk as violent and negative. New Punks were attracted to the movement without violent tendencies, but without Punk tendencies either. "As more and more people adopt the appearance of Punk, they have less and less of an idea of its content. The critical message of Punk has a number of targets including classism, sexism, racism, and authoritarianism.... When 'punks' adopt the form or style without attention to the critical message of the Punk movement, people's assumptions about racism, sexism, classism, and authoritarianism remain unchallenged; the seeds of the Punk movement's own destruction are sown" (Larry Zbach, MRR).

It is true that many Punks are violent, fashionable, apathetic teenagers. It is also true that Punks are not this way on the whole and the media misrepresentations have harmed the movement by increasing its ignorance factor. For the Punks who are not attracted to nor dismayed by their media portrayal, the movement offers a place to create their own culture and concentrate on what they feel is important. These people "are more valuable to the human gene pool than the 'normal' members of their generation because they're more intelligent, curious, daring, defiant, critical, active, ambitious and determined than the rest of their demographic, who seem to be chasing the latest perversion of the American Dream with the same zombie fervor displayed by Ron Cobb's famous cartoon character stumbling through the post-holocaust rubble, broken TV set under his arm, plug extended in hand, searching shell-shocked for a functioning outlet" (Jonathan Formula, Hardcore California, 6).

Perhaps the greatest damage the media has done to the American Punk Rock scene has been the linkage between Punks and Skinheads. While a fairly understandable mistake, both Punks and Skinheads often have crew cut hair and attend similar concerts, the rise in Skinhead violence and racism have done great damage to the Punk scene. This problem has not been as great in the UK because Skinheads had their own culture years before Punk appeared and maintain it rather separately today.

ANTI-RACIST ACTION

THE ONLY GOOD FASCIST ...IS A DEAD ONE

CRO-MAGS

CRO-MAGS NYC

AGNOSTIC FRONT

DEATH BEFORE DISHONOR SDP

SUNDAY MATINEE OCT 14 CBGB

STOP RACISM

Skrewdriver

White Power

ARYAN NATIONS

NEW YORK CITY HATE-CORE

NAZI SKINHEADS GET OUT!

SMASH RACISM

18

California Über Alles

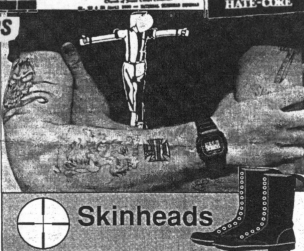

Skinheads

SKINHEADS AND RACISM
WHO THEY ARE, WHERE THEY'RE FROM AND WHAT DO THEY HAVE TO DO WITH PUNK ANYWAY.

"What's the difference between Punks and Skins? We're all in the same scene, all listening to the same music. It's all about thrashing the government, the people that hold you down" (Carl, a San Francisco Skinhead, MRR #18, Oct. 1984).

During the early eighties the differences between American Punks and Skinheads (or Skins) were fairly small. Skinheads were definitely more conformist, violent, and politically apathetic than Punks, but were nowhere near the racist, white power supporters they are commonly portrayed as. Skinheads did little to support the growing Punk scenes other than attending (and often ruining) concerts of Punk bands. That they shared the same musical tastes and often the same haircuts (shaved heads) enabled the media and ignorant spectators to lump them together. This has proven a large mistake because of the growing radical politics of Punks and the equally growing racism and ignorance of Skinheads. The middle and late eighties showed Skinheads to be the enemies of a constructive Punk scene with constant violence at concerts and ties to racist organizations. Here I will give a brief background of who the Skinheads are, their common attitudes on racism and patriotism, and how these stances are contrary to the politics and philosophy of Punk.

The specific roots of the Skinhead movement are pretty much agreed upon. There have been many books written on its history due to the recent surge in the Skinhead popularity amongst teens. STP (Skinhead Times Publishing) in Scotland publishes a variety of both fiction and nonfiction titles of interest to the Skinhead cult and Punks as well. I highly recommend searching them out. For a well documented history complete with clippings, photos and personal text, read George Marshall's <u>Spirit of '69—a Skinhead Bible</u>.

"The origins of the movement came from black Jamaican music—the music which came in the form of reggae and soul and later in ska—and was exported to England and shared with white working class people. It was always a multi-racial thing and always imbedded with working class politics which are very much against racism" (Kieran, of Anti-Racist Action (A.R.A.), <u>MRR</u> #78, Nov. 1989).

These original Skins in England's early sixties were not anti-black, but were still tarnished with racism. There was "an influx of Pakistani immigrants into England in the mid-60's, providing a cheap labor force. Factory owners found it much easier to exploit the ignorant immigrants" (Ken Cousino, <u>MRR</u> #42, Nov. 1986). This resulted in the unemployment of many of the Skinheads and their parents. The combination of boredom, poverty, and frustration, provoked Skins to direct their anger at the new immigrant workers. "The Skins would go on raids, brutalizing, and sometimes killing, Pakistanis whose only crime was being in the wrong place at the wrong time" (ibid). This displaced anger and immigrant scapegoating is ongoing throughout Europe and the United States today.

When the Punk explosion occurred in England, the Skinheads replaced their Jamaican ska music with Punk Rock and entered a new stage. The early anger and aggression of the original Punks attracted Skins to the concerts that they would eventually wreck with their own brand of patriotic, drunken violence. Skins formed bands as well and sang of losing jobs to foreigners and the pride they took in being English working class. While these bands exhibited much less skill than even the earliest of Punk bands, they became quickly popular amongst both the working class and the organizations who saw that they could exploit them. Fascist organizations such as the National Front funded Skinhead bands in order to draw new members and use them as "soldiers" in acts of harassment and violence. By 1978-79, the English Skinheads had "their own uniform, music, and a new philosophy based on soccer, pubs, racism and fascism" (ibid).

Many of these Skinhead bands eventually lost interest in Punk and returned to playing the original Skinhead music of ska. As a result, the English Skins have become much less visible in the Punk scene and more concerned with their own original music and fashion. The Skinheads of England are not much of a threat to Punks (and seem less of a threat to Pakistanis than before) and are looked upon as a subculture of young people who idealize the past (the sixties) of their long standing movement.

Philadelphia, Pa, '88

Just as American Punks copied ideas and styles from the English, the American Skinhead came about with ideas based on the English example of the late '70's. The American Skinhead has many traits similar to and different from his English counterpart. American Skins adopted the same clothing and blind patriotism from the English while preferring the newer, faster American Hardcore music. American Skins were primarily middle class white teens who had little reason to be racist or unemployed. They were basically rebellious kids who liked to drink and fight, both of which could be done at Punk shows of the early eighties. Not until 1985-87 did American Skinheads begin to show the ugliness of their English predecessors.

The media played a large role in drawing racists and reactionary rednecks to the Skinhead movement and making a fairly harmless and stupid trend into a real problem. Skinheads recruited by white supremacist organizations similar to the UK's National Front made frequent appearances on talk shows, talking tough and compelling many youths to join. Skinheads became very popular due to an image of machoness and "street smarts." Although the situation was much different from England, Skinhead teens were convinced that Americans of African, Asian, or Hispanic backgrounds (as compared to Pakistanis in England) were taking "their" jobs without looking at the reality of the situation.

Even the Skins who did not become admirers of Hitler-esque politics or get white power tattoos became reactionary, more violent and even more numerous than before. Among this second group were some black, Asian and Hispanic Skinheads who were as equally ignorant and violent as the Nazi Skins but conveniently maintained an anti-racist stance.

While the trend grew throughout the country, being more racist and violent in some areas (San Diego, Portland, Boston, Florida...) than others, high school bullies donned the traditional Skinhead uniform (Doc Marten work boots, flight jackets, suspenders) and became a menace. Hate crimes and abuse of homeless people became common Skinhead activities. While this was going on, the Skins maintained their association with the Punk scene by ruining shows with fights and vandalism. This could be blamed on the Punk communities that were often too weak to stand up for themselves, allowing a small number of bullies to intimidate an entire crowd.

Pro-War Duck Hunter, '91

These events led to the general idea that Punk and Skin unity is ridiculous or at least completely undesirable. Most Skinheads are right wing, homophobic, white middle class males. There are exceptions to this, but there are few exceptions to the Skinheads' blind patriotism to whichever country they inhabit. Part of the American Skinhead uniform is to wear the American (or confederate) flag on the shoulder of his/her flight jacket. The protests surrounding the Gulf War often had the Skinheads alongside their ignorant peers challenging protesters to fight and hurling racial and sexist insults. With such patriotic fervor it is surprising that they were not more willing to enlist in the military while eagerly condemning those resisting war. Punks are most likely to reject patriotism as both unnecessary and dangerous. This has caused problems between Punks and Skins many times.

Many confrontations have occurred between Punks and Skins on the occasions of flag burnings and at concerts and events featuring politically active Punk bands and their followers. I have witnessed several S.H.A.R.P. (Skinheads Against Racial Prejudice) Skins assault and batter a fellow protester at an anti-KKK rally for burning a flag. This group contained black and female members. In NYC on July Fourth, 1989 around fifty Skinheads stopped a flag burning by leftist groups and Punks in Washington Square Park. "The Skinheads chanted, 'Burn the flag and we'll burn a fag,' called Abbie Hoffman an 'asshole,' and shouted, 'This is America—love it or leave it.'" (MRR #76, Sept. 1989). At least one Punk was brutally beaten by these Skinheads.

Later in the day, Skinheads went to Tompkins Square Park where a number of Punks had gathered to confront them. The police interceded before any fighting occurred. The police were not so concerned earlier in the afternoon when the Skinheads smashed a Punk operated Anarchist center destroying the storefront and hospitalizing one man.

The New York City area had the largest (or at least the most visible/influential) Skinhead scene in the United States during 1984-88. The bands that came from NYC were mostly unoriginal, bald, violence-glorifying Skins with reactionary politics. They lacked the tuneful sing-a-long anthems of their UK counterparts and replaced it with a brand of tuneless thrash. They were not Nazis, but certainly did not share radical politics with the Punks. The largest American Skinhead band has been NYC's **Agnostic Front**. Many of the other Skinhead bands have been influenced by their words and music since 1982. Like other New York bands, their lyrics are mostly made up of macho bravado and pride in one's self, city, and country. On homosexuals, "I don't beat up gay guys, but let them stay on the West Side. If I see a guy rubbing his crotch and licking his lips, I'll put him out. I have friends who are, but I don't want to know what they do" (**Agnostic Front**, Flipside #45, 1985). An attitude encouraging homophobia and macho strength became part of the Skinhead ideology and spread to New York's emerging Straight Edge scene who shared the same clubs and favorite bands as the Skinheads.

Agnostic Front and other Skinhead bands spoke out regularly against communists, anarchists, and others who they saw as "liberal groups." These groups "brainwash so easy. They brainwash all these kids into this world peace stuff which will never exist.... Telling you to support the Third World, man, stuff like that" (ibid). Other Skinheads have echoed this ignorant rightist view by aiming criticism at Punks. "Can't you Punkers see you are living in the freest nation in the world? Who cares about a war 2,000 miles away? It's not in America. As for nukes: it's better to die a free man than to live a hundred years as a slave to the Russians.... I am a Rightist and hate liberals, communists, gays (because they are perverts), and they should all be annihilated.... Most of all I hate Punks because they represent communism, gay, and are totally stupid people" (Carmelo Nieves, MRR #18, Oct. 1984). It is easy to see

Bender U.K., Ft. Lauderdale, Fl, '95

from the earlier quotes who the "stupid people" really are.

There are Skinheads who are gay, communist, liberal, and non-violent. They, in essence, subscribe to no Skinhead principles other than wearing the uniform, as it has become a large fashion trend in the United States. Indeed one cannot walk through the gay ghettos without seeing dozens of uniformed "skinheads." I am not referring to them in this section. These folks can argue until blue in the face about the slagging "good skins" receive, but I can only wonder why they would label themselves Skinheads in 1990's America.

Again, not all Skinheads are Nazis or even racist at all. In fact the largest opposition to racist Skinheads has been from other Skinheads. These non-racist Skins wear the same uniform as the others but hold slightly different beliefs on what it means to be a Skinhead. They accept and acknowledge non-white Skins but are often just as patriotic and violent as their peers. Groups such as S.H.A.R.P., A.R.A. (Anti-Racist Action), and other local groups of

Skinheads have formed to dismiss the racist Skinhead stereotype. How exactly do they stop racist Skinheads? "From our experience the tactic that has worked in Minneapolis includes physical confrontation. Which is fighting them and kicking the shit out of them" (Kieran of A.R.A., MRR #78). A similar group in Britain, Anti-Fascist Action, believes in fighting the Nazis "by the only language they understand—by boots, fists, iron bars and whatever else it takes to show these clowns that we are not fucking around and will not tolerate attacks on people because of their race, sexual preference, sex or political beliefs" (Frank Hughs, MRR #103, Dec 1991).

Anti-racist Skinhead groups have been criticized on two major points. The first is their commitment to violence which many see as an excuse to flex their muscles without being condemned. When people question their tactics the typical response is, "I think the non-violent approach is kind of unrealistic. I don't think it works. We can look historically and herstorically at pacifist movements and see actually what works" (Jonna of A.R.A., PE #13). The pacifist approach is deemed as not only impractical, but potentially racist. "I think that a lot of white liberals who talk about pacifism can be construed as pretty racist, or classist, or sexist because of those positions of power white middle class people find themselves in" (ibid). Or when people condemn their violent tactics, "I think that's really fucked up and I think there's some racist attitudes to that" (Kieran). It should be noted that Kieran is currently being charged with assault in Minneapolis for supposedly attacking a racist at a rally. Knowing his tactics, it is not surprising that either he did assault someone, or else he is an easy target to be framed by the cowardly racist involved. Of course, I hope that the charge is dropped and Kieran can continue his dedicated fight against racism being more careful of his actions when the pigs are near.

The other point of criticism anti-racists find themselves confronted with is their view on freedom of speech.

"The speech that fascists speak is preaching geno-
cide and hate, and that is not about freedom, that is not
about liberation, it is about killing people and subordina-
tion and domination and perpetuating a hierarchy. The
kind of free speech I want to be a part of is empowering
everybody and liberation for everybody and I don't feel
that by allowing fascists to speak, this is going to create
true freedom for everybody. The people that invite fascists
to speak on the radio or anywhere, I think that should be
disrupted and not allowed to happen because it's not building towards true liberation" (Jonna).

It is true that fascist speech is not building towards
liberation. The problem is that physical violence against
those with differing opinions, regardless of how harmful or
ridiculous, is certainly a form of censorship that is potentially harmful and detrimental to a free society. It is easy to
see how good intentions backed by willing violence can be
twisted into a dangerous and misguided movement, censor-
ing anything deemed racist or fascist. If anything, the censorship of this moronic right-wing crap has made it even
more popular among the moronic followers of the genre.
Claiming underground, persecuted, and censored status has
led to the steady proliferation of white power skinhead
garbage that would never have sold on its own (lack of)
merits.

Skinheads in America have, by and large, become
nothing but a youth trend. Their only threat is to the Punk
community with whom there are still fights at larger concerts. Although the majority of American Skinheads are not
racist anymore, they are still mostly patriotic, ignorant bullies. Punks and Skinheads have almost nothing in common
(with the exception of Straight Edge Punks who have
adopted the Skins clean cut look and often conservative
views) but are constantly lumped together due to similar
musical tastes. This shows that Skins must not actually
read or understand the lyrics of many of the Punk bands
they support.

Scared of Chaka, Tucson, Az, '95

In the past, few Punk bands have been brave enough to speak out against Skinheads at their shows due to the threat of violence, but this is changing. There are cases of some towns having shows without allowing Skins to enter, and other cases of clubs making it clear that they will not tolerate Skins' mindless violence. The ABC No Rio club in

New York must be mentioned for their accomplishment in changing New York City's reputation from a violent Skinhead/Straight Edge scene into one that is now a creative and politically active Punk scene. Shows that would have been fight-filled contests years ago are now practically Skinhead free and places for fun and communication. The American scene seems to be turning away from Skinheads on a whole, and I do not think that Skins will be making a large comeback any time soon into the younger Punk Rock scene.

Most of the information on Skinheads and other topics in this book can not be found in mainstream

Soulside, Annville, Pa, '87

publications or in libraries. Media sources distort and sensationalize Skinheads' and Punks' philosophies because they do not have sufficient knowledge on the subjects. To get to the truth of the matters at hand, one requires primary sources. The primary sources for this book come in the forms of personal experiences and from reading fanzines.

Swingin Utters, Pueblo, Co, '95

INTRA MOVEMENT COMMUNICATION:
FANZINES–COMMUNICATION FROM THE XEROX MACHINE TO THE UNDERGROUND.

"My own breakdown of major zine types would go like this (not in any particular order): art (including comics, mail art, collage stuff), conservative-Constitutionalist, ecological-environmental, film (mostly horror-sleaze-gore), poetry, religion (pagan-subgenius Discordian-ceremonial magic), anarchist-leftist, music, science fiction-fantasy, mainstream literary, UFO-Fortean-psychic-odd science-cranks-peace-anti-war-socially conscious, gay-lesbian-bisexual. Probably 90% of what's being published in the small press can be put (maybe with some forcing) into one of those categories" (Mike Gunderloy, editor of Factsheet Five, MRR #77, Oct. 1989).

The Punk fanzines (or zines for short) are the primary form of communication amongst Punks. They are put out by Punks for Punks and cover an extremely large spectrum of topics. In this book I have been and will be using the larger fanzines (usually a circulation over one thousand copies is a large fanzine) for most of the information. The larger ones usually are based on both music and politics with only a smattering of interest in the other topics mentioned above. This is not to say that the others are not interesting, fun or inspiring because they do not deal directly with the Punk world, but that they are not too useful for this discussion. Fanzines made up of poetry or

FANZINE of the month

BEN IS DEAD

PROFANE EXISTENCE

MAKING PUNK A THREAT AGAIN!

Surf Kuwait

MAXIMUM ROCKNROLL

CLASS WAR

BRITAINS MOST UNRULY TABLOID

SEARCH & DESTROY

The original, undiluted magazine that the others copied. We still have a few of the 1977-78 issues left. They contain incendiary interviews and passionate photographic. Corrosive concentrated encapsulation of the only youth rebellion of the seventies: punk rock; the philosophy and culture, before the mass media take-over and inevitable cloning.

SEARCH & DESTROY

LOS ANGELES FLIP SIDE

EULOGY

PUNK ROC
PERMS
CLASH
MORE

NEW!

panopticon

Assault With Intent

To F.

RAISING HELL

20p

BASTARDS!

Toxik Ephex, Scraps,
Christ On Parade

MAXIMUM ROCKNRO

HEY KIDS!

Get your official

in time for Christmas

TRUST

Europe's biggest regularly magazine. send all records notes, articles etc. to: AN

No. 164

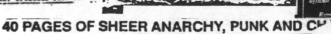

40 PAGES OF SHEER ANARCHY, PUNK AND CL

photographs capture the art and experiences of Punks equally well, but are hard to convey in words. "As a unified body of work, the Punk fanzines provide an overall view, a synthesis of the various elements—music, philosophy, aesthetics, and attitude—that make up the phenomenon of Punk" (Henry, 95).

Fanzines came about in the mid-70's with the growth of the Punk scenes in New York and London. The largest fanzines at this time were Sniffin' Glue from England and Punk from New York. Like most fanzines they were short lived, had small circulations (by professional magazine standards), and had a very amateurish (again, by glossy magazine standards) approach to publishing. Fanzines should not be confused with magazines that have glossy covers, full color pages, and high budgets. Most fanzines are done on copy machines and stapled together without page numbers, copyrights or chances of making money. To be a fanzine editor all one needs is an urge to express her own opinion, ideas or thoughts and access to a cheap copy machine. Fanzines are sold primarily through the mail, as stores will seldom carry products with such a small profit margin and so small an audience. By the time the two fanzines mentioned earlier folded, they had already influenced enough people to begin a network of locally based fanzines that would soon connect a worldwide Punk network.

The fanzine craze gained strength quickly in the early California scene where "an essential part of the scene were the fanzines, Xeroxed or mimeographed papers featuring the bands and their followers. Flipside came out of Whittier, cost a quarter and featured a nasty, trashy, authentically teenage look at the scene and its fans. Flipside was the younger, cruder side of Slash. Slash was always a bit intellectual, while Flipside was just straight-forward, dumb fun" (Craig Lee, Hardcore California, 18). With the demise of Slash, Flipside soon grew to be the largest of the Southern Californian zines. While still focusing on the local area, Flipside became one of the first to interview Punks from different parts of Europe. Flipside has since become less and less concerned with Punk and is now mostly a "new music" magazine with the original editors offering little input to the magazine. Nevertheless, with their slogan of "be more than a witness," Flipside showed the entire country and Europe that anyone could and should do it themselves.

Coming out of San Francisco in 1982, Maximum Rock N Roll added a fanzine to their thriving Punk radio show bringing more politics and different scenes into view than Flipside previously had done. With a focus on not only California, but the entire country and world, MRR printed "scene reports" written by readers from around the globe. Printing advertisements and addresses for contacts and music from all fifty states, South America, Japan, Europe (East and West), and even the Soviet Union, MRR helped to build a truly worldwide Punk community.

MRR has outlasted every major American fanzine except for Flipside and has used their emphasis on egalitarian politics to help shape the views of thousands of Punks throughout the years. While taking much criticism for defining "what Punk

Kilkare, Fairfield, Ca, '98

is," the editor, Tim Yohannon, has never claimed to be an objective publisher. In reaction to the <u>Flipside</u> editors questioning his censorship of an advertisement for a racist skinhead band: "I don't like to give space to attitudes which I feel are really reactionary and add to a growing stupidity. As far as an 'alternative,' and as a fanzine, which by definition is done by individuals, I feel that the zine should be a reflection of what those individuals want. We're not the only fanzine in the world, and we're not trying to pretend that we're some kind of objective thing.... I just don't want to contribute in any way to the growth of that (racist skinhead) mentality" (Tim Yohannon, <u>MRR</u> #49, June 1987).

<u>MRR</u> has had a continual turnover in staff members and has grown larger and larger in the past few years. Updated computer equipment has given it a more professional look (although still black and white), and an increase in submissions (95% of the fanzine) has doubled

Los Crudos, Corpus Christi, Tx, '95

its length to more than 150 pages (still unnumbered). While still receiving criticism for promoting specific politics, the majority of legitimate criticism comes from those who feel that <u>MRR</u> has too much power over the Punk scene. It is true that a whole segment of Punks agree entirely with what <u>MRR</u> prints (often without a healthy dose of doubt or humor), and that a good record or fanzine review from their volunteer staff insures good sales. Too many Punks now depend on <u>MRR</u> to inform them of who to support and who to boycott, and while I would agree with the majority of their views, their new found power is extremely dangerous and sometimes abused by the columnists and staff whose opinions have a very great influence on younger Punks.

Despite the complaints about and drawbacks of <u>MRR</u>, it has done an extremely good job of accomplishing its goals on a monthly basis. These goals or main ideas are "(l) To provide a forum for progressive attitudes within the Punk/Hardcore scene. (2) To provide a vehicle for the ongoing growth of grass roots activity. (3) To provide a documentation of the changes internationally that affect us politically, socially and culturally" (Tim Yohannon, <u>PE</u> #3, 8). Regardless of criticisms and the occasional apathetic moods of the Punk scene, Yohannon feels that <u>MRR</u>: "Will keep trying to connect people, will continue to be activist, and will always keep trying to move people towards positive actions. We can't do it ourselves, but by maintaining certain principles of integrity (like not drawing salary, or by publishing our finances), we can perhaps demonstrate by example. And we can be activists by dreaming up and organizing such projects as <u>MRR</u> radio, Blacklist Mailorder (a now defunct volunteer mail-order service that carried almost any and all Punk records and fanzines), Gilman Street Project (a warehouse which holds weekly all age Punk shows), Pressure Drop Press (the publisher of <u>Threat By Example</u>, a Noam Chomsky book, <u>Sabotage in the American Workplace</u>, and <u>You Don't Have to Fuck People Over to Survive</u>), and Epicenter (a record store and fanzine library). These are all not-for-profit, DIY (do it yourself) enterprises committed to strengthening communication and under-underground economic clout" (Tim Yohannon, MRR #100, Sept. 1991). As MRR does cover the worldwide scene and contains views and submissions from Punks all over the world, I feel justified in using it as a main source for information concerning the thoughts and actions of the current Punk scene.

The more radical alternative to MRR is the Minneapolis fanzine Profane Existence. PE is anarchist oriented and deals more with politics and political bands than either Flipside or MRR. It began in late 1989 and for the first ten issues had a layout exactly like MRR's 8.5 x 11 size, though it was much shorter in length. For unexplained reasons, PE temporarily abandoned this format for a newspaper tabloid layout modeled after the popular left newspapers. Luckily for us readers the editors have switched back to the old format with expanded contents. PE has grown to be one of the largest fanzines and, due to its openly aggressive politics, has gained large audience responses from Europe. The staff are very obviously influenced by the early British political Punks and seem to be very committed individuals. When this book was printed, PE had only been out for three years. Since then it has definitely become second only to MRR in influence and popularity amongst Punks. The editors "publish each issue with the intent of spreading word of our own activities as well as to be a resource for those involved with anarchist and/or Punk culture and activism. We also publish with the intent of crossing the barriers of alienation which keep society as a whole separated and pacified. If our politics or attitudes somehow offend you... tough shit!" (PE #13, Jan. 1992, 1).

Although Flipside, MRR and PE are certainly not the only fanzines read throughout North America and Europe, they have certainly been the most influential. Each European country has its own collection of large and small fanzines, but these are primarily written in the country's language and feature more local coverage. These three are read in many other countries and offer coverage of foreign happenings. These and other fanzines have not only served to report the attitudes and actions of the Punk scene, but to determine its course as well. There have been thousands of different fanzines produced over the last twenty years. Using these three as the main sources was done out of the availability and acceptance which each has gained within the Punk scene.

It is important here to update some changes in the zine world. First off, a zine explosion has occurred both in the quantity and popularity of zines. Major distributors and chain stores have started to accept zines for sale and display on news racks all over America. For many zines this is a fantastic chance to reach a larger audience or for the kid living in Hicktown, PA, the opportunity to meet underground culture. The negative side being that zines often feel the pressure to become more "professional" or mainstream in order to gain mass acceptance. There is certainly a huge glut of carbon copy Punker zines on the market taking up shelf space at Tower records. Professionally designed and made up entirely of ads, reviews, and boring interviews, these losers show none of the creativity or heart of their rougher, more passionate predecessors. Also, books on zines have become commonplace, as have large format books by zinesters chronicling out of print issues of zines.

Earlier this year Tim Yohannon died, leaving the course of MRR in the hands of a younger less experienced crew. Hopefully this crew will not forget Tim's legacy of forging a rebellious social message into the magazine which now promotes a very narrow band of Punk music. In 1999 Profane Existence will cease publication. This will create a huge gap in an already sparse Anarchist Punk scene. Luckily, they have left us with a fine book entitled Making Punk a Threat Again. Pick it up.

It is important to remember that however large or small fanzines are, they all have the same goal: communication of the ideas which define Punk culture and philosophy. Thus, fanzines can be used to show the specifics on ideas such as anarchy, sex-related issues, environmental philosophies, and the politics of Punk business.

ANARCHISM: AN ALTERNATIVE TO EXISTING SYSTEMS. WHAT IT IS AND WHY IT IS EMBRACED BY PUNKS ALL OVER THE WORLD. THE FAILURE OF "BOUGHT AND PAID FOR" POLITICIANS HAS ENSURED A COUNTERCULTURE RECEPTIVE TO THE IDEA THAT WE WOULD BE BETTER OFF WITHOUT THESE VAMPIRES.

**"All government is undesirable and unnec-
essary. There are no services provided by the
state that the community could not provide
itself. We don't need anyone telling us what to
do, trying to run our lives, harassing us with
taxes, rules, regulations, and living high on the
hog off our labor"** (Anarchist Youth Federation
(AYF), <u>Profane Existence</u> **#5**, Aug. 1990, 38).

When it comes to choosing a political ideology,
Punks are primarily anarchists. There are few who promote
the continuation of any form of capitalism or communism.
This is not to say that all Punks are well read in the history and theory of anarchism, but most do share a belief
formed around the anarchist principles of having no official government or rulers, and valuing individual freedom
and responsibility (who doesn't). The Minneapolis based
fanzine, <u>Profane Existence</u>, is the largest of the anarchist
Punk fanzines in North America and contains both music
and politics reported from an anarchist perspective. There
are many other valuable periodicals that are aimed at more
intellectually/activist inclined readers and those which
have left out the musical side of the Punk movement for a
politics-only format.

The European scene has had a larger amount of
anarchist fanzines and bands, resulting in the European
Punks historically being more politically active than their
North American counterparts. The creators and editors of
these fanzines were influenced by the second wave of
European Punk (1980-84) which was visibly politically ori-
ented. These bands such as **Crass**, **Conflict**, and
Discharge in the UK, **The Ex** and **BGK** in Holland, and
MDC and **Dead Kennedys** in America, changed many
Punks into rebellious thinkers rather than just Rock 'n'
Rollers. The ideologies of these bands are carried on today
by groups playing at all ends of Punk's musical spectrum.
The blazing political thrash of Chicago's **Los Crudos**

screams in the face of oppression just as the explicit class conscious lyrics of **Propagandhi** find a perfect home in sing-a-long pop Punk. The result of these bands are thousands of young people calling themselves "anarchists" and holding a healthy contempt for the present governing regimes.

"Early in the development of what we call civilization a few folks realized that they could live easily and grow rich by making other people work for them. These people used cunning or brute force to institute themselves as chieftains, shamans, kings or priests. Through threats and superstition they kept people in line. Now and then their subjects would revolt and they would either grant enough reform to placate them or be replaced by a new ruler. Such is the nature of government" (Felix, "Professor Felix's Very Short History of Anarchism," Profane Existence #1, Dec. 1989, 13).

Punks have turned to anarchism as an alternative to the world's existing systems and the continual cycle of oppression each revolution brings. The nature of governments (and hierarchies in general) involves oppression and exploitation of the people living under it (or affected by it). Unlike other youth or bourgeois countercultures, Punks reject communism and the left wing of traditional democratic governments as well as capitalism. Reforms made by ruling parties are often condemned as stateist (favoring the maintenance of a formal government) and superficial. Reforms are granted to appease and not to free the people involved. Regarding communism, many Punks have been in agreement with the movement's supposed support of women's rights, the working class, and a shared distaste for capitalist society. Many members of the Punk community have taken part in demonstrations organized by the Sparticist League, the Revolutionary Communist Party (RCP), and other Marxist /Leninist/Trotskyist groups because they appeared to have similar goals involving specific issues. Anarchists and anyone who reads history, realize that the realities of communism have been far from the goals of an ideal anarchist state.

"Communist groups, when out of power, talk a different line altogether. They present communism as a noble force fighting for equality and justice against oppression and domination of the capitalists. But the fact is that the left wing parties are authoritarian by nature. Any system which holds as part of its philosophy the domination of one human by another holds the possibility of oppression. Communist groups are not struggling for the liberation of the masses but for their own rise to power. Once in power they adopt the same repressive means to maintain it that all governments do" (Felix and Rat, "Revolt Against Communism," PE #2, Feb. 1990, 22).

Cited evidence to back up the oppressiveness of communism comes not only from the current repressive

Washington, D.C., '91

regimes, but also the Kronstadt uprising of 1921, the Ukrainian Anarchist movement of 1918-21, and the Spanish Civil War of 1936-39 where anarchists were betrayed and crushed by totalitarian communist forces. Communist regimes are not necessarily different in their subsequent results than the overthrown regime, at least not to the subjects being ruled. Revolution is not meant to be a simple exchange of rulers. "In this century, revolution has come to mean an engineered revolution by a professional class of communist organizers that have merely overthrown capitalist systems and replaced them with equally or more oppressive ones of their own" (Minnesota band **Destroy**, PE #1, 29). In this sense, revolutions have become a vicious circle, the discontented revolt only to create a new class of discontented. Communism does not have the desired degrees of freedom afforded with anarchism and so should not be any more favorable than its supposed enemy, capitalism.

The Punk movement was originally formed in nations holding capitalist, pseudo-democratic policies. Because of this, capitalism and its problems became the first target of political Punks. Homelessness, classism, and work place exploitation seem to be some of the results of a system built on greed. While it is true that a capitalist system affords great luxuries to many members of its society, this seems to have a direct link to the exploitation of those who do not have these luxuries. The long held belief of becoming rich through honest hard work has been continually debunked. If this was so, many of the current lower class, including my family and myself, would be filthy rich.

In a capitalist society the definition of success has been written in terms of wealth and commodities. Using this definition, the middle class is "well off" enough to resist any kind of radical change, content with their status and fearful of becoming "poor." Even the materially poor, who should (and often do) realize their true situation, work for a chance to engage in middle class luxuries. The fact that people loot stereos and televisions instead of food shows that they have been convinced that a better life is more money and more goods.

There is no doubt that certain luxuries and money can make life easier, but to judge success and failure on such terms has dangerous implications. "Capitalism relies on a theoretical model that assumes that everybody is out to maximize their individual profit. And by and large, human beings have conformed to the model, turning all the things around them into commodities which can be bought and sold" ("New World Order," MRR #98, July 1991). This is most evident in the current dangers and disasters facing the environment. When economists calculate the value of environmental products without measuring the loss involved, they insure disaster for our future generations of humans and our current generation of plants and animals. In a more extreme case, "this thinking reaches its peak in times of war where people and human combat all

Ruin, Baltimore, Md, '86

become commodities; killing loses its meaning" (ibid). This is a very important point and the Gulf War in the Middle East can be used to stress this example.

It has been said time and time again that capitalism is cannibalism. This statement is usually used when referring to how corporate owners or executives exploit their fellow humans in the desire to make profit. Capitalism often seems to thrive on the misery of some group of people. During the Gulf War the soldiers of both sides were used as tools that not only prevented profit loss, but increased business. "Certain facts surrounding the war are indisputable: hundreds of thousands of innocent people lost their lives; a civilization was destroyed. In capitalist

Stratford Mercenaries, Bayview SF, '97

America, the war took on quite different implications: there was a lot of money to be made" (ibid). Without going into the obvious reasons of why the war was wrong and unjustifiable (if any war can actually be justified), we can look at some of the economic results of the war. Desert Storm shirts, videos, television specials, and bumper stickers capitalized on the racist slogans and the deaths of many to sell products. The oil companies were perhaps the greatest "winners" in the profit category, and the popular anti-war slogan, "no blood for oil," would have been more accurate as, "no blood for profits."

The total cost of the war to the United States has been estimated at sixty billion dollars. (This does not include the losses of allied lives, however many there were, and certainly does not include the losses of Iraq.) If we are to use this figure as accurate, which would be a moral crime, we can see further evidence of American profits. "With the allied contribution standing at $57 billion, and with the $18 billion in advance payments from Saudi Arabia and Kuwait for new arms sales, this war will turn out to have been a money-making venture for the United States government" (ibid). Not only the government, but large corporate construction companies will be increasing their bank accounts by rebuilding Iraq. The more damage, the more rebuilding, the more profits.

It seems perverse to profit from war, but it does happen. Is it too far-fetched to think that some would be eager for war to boost the economy and personal profits, decrease unemployment and raise patriotic fervor, all under the guise of a stated military objective? "Some would construct elaborate conspiracy theories to explain phenomena like this, but in our opinion none are needed. The truth is far more insidious: to profit from war is a rational act in a capitalist system that turns everything into a commodity whose only value is determined by the 'free market'" (ibid). Thus capitalism, as far as its basis lies in the dehumanization and exploitation of people (and perhaps even animals/the natural environment) for wealth, cannot be

77

accepted by anarchists. There are several other reasons for anarchists to reject capitalism and the pseudo-democratic state. Some of these shall be seen later.

Anarchist Punks appear to hold many beliefs that agree with what can be termed the radical, liberal or far left wings of democracy. Beliefs in defending women's rights, racial equality, and gay rights are involved in the platforms of both the liberal and the anarchist. These similarities, however, are not enough to keep the anarchist from condemning the Left as much as (or even more than) the Right. "It seems strange that anarchists can enter into coalition and work with left wing groups. In reality anarchism is just as opposed to leftist politics as it is to right wing groups" (Felix and Rat, PE #2). Again the Gulf War can be used to illustrate the differences between the Left and the anarchists.

The protests and resistance efforts of the Left showed its unwillingness to "take a principled stand in favor of radical egalitarianism" ("New World Order," MRR #99, Aug. 1991). In general, the view that anarchists have of the Left is that it is afraid of doing anything "that might bring it into direct confrontation with the State" (ibid). I personally attended the larger of the two anti-war protests in Washington D.C. and can verify the anarchists' claim. The protest was set up by several liberal groups who made a point to promote themselves and sell their merchandise. "Movement leaders essentially called on demonstrators to fall in line behind the sloganeers, to rattle their chains 'like civilized people' rather than risk breaking them. Marchers were told to stay on the sidewalk and behave for the media; spontaneous, creative opposition was discouraged. And for those who had a different vision, there were 'peace monitors' to keep everyone in line" (ibid).

The process of coalition building may sometimes result in a broad based protest addressing a number of issues which can be shown as interrelated. In this case, it seemed merely to water down the message of the protest.

In order to not offend any of the groups present (except the communist group who was offensive in their ridiculous vocal support for Iraq), the message of the protest movement became "Bring Our Troops Home Now!" While not meaning to devalue a human life, many Punks went on to adopt the more poignant slogan "Fuck the Troops." Supporting the soldiers to destroy and kill or to bring them home so that they (as opposed to less valuable soldiers) are not endangered involves a limited and flawed perception of the situation. "Protesters reduced the war to a single, easily digested issue: the military is OK, just not this war. In this way the peace movement underscored the patriotic lies of the mainstream, framing their opposition in terms of an alternative national interest: 'Peace is Patriotic!' Anyone really interested in peace should reject patriotism and understand that this country is founded on oppression and exploitation" (ibid). It should be obvious by now that Punks are not very patriotic at all. "For me to be patriotic and opposed to the majority, I would be a hypocrite. I see it as impossible to support this country's good points without supporting its bad. Whenever the subject of death, torture, and neglect becomes a reality due to this country, then in my eyes, mind, and heart, the bad points definitely outweigh the good" (Martin Sprouse, MRR #39, Aug. 1986).

The protests and the entire approach to the war by the Left seemed to promote a general feeling of helplessness and individual powerlessness. The only way to oppose the war was to join a group and then leave power to the leaders of the group. The media was only interested in the few statements given from the leaders or celebrities. The only thing a person could do was buy a T-shirt or write a letter. For the Left, methods of protest are pre-defined and the rules strictly adhered to. "Lines of authority, hierarchy, and profit-making were thus maintained without any recognition of the ways in which these forces were responsible for the Gulf conflict: the order obeying private would have felt right at home. The message of these protests was clear: tell them you're angry (in the meekest of terms) then go home and watch TV" ("New World Order," MRR #99,.Aug. 1991).

The characteristics and failures of the Gulf resistance are common parts of the Left. The anarchist is turned off by the domineering techniques and attitudes of Leftist leaders towards their followers and by the members' eagerness to blindly accept authority. "The formal Left is dominated by single issue, careerist professionals who stifle change through bureaucracy and petty status struggles, all too often masquerading as professionalism" (ibid). Similar to the communists, the Left seeks out the discontented "funnelling them into the tedium of drumming up votes for 'progressive' politicians who will invariably sell them out, or collecting signatures for legislation that won't be enforced, even if passed" (ibid). Anyone who has taken the time to work for non-profit "cause" motivated groups for a living can vouch for the truth of this. Obviously there has been some good done by the democratic Left, but the anarchist looks on these measures as only appeasement, not real changes. The most basic criticism with left wing politics is that they seek change by working within a system that is already corrupt and destructive. However good the proposal for improvement may be, the anarchist will be content with nothing but total change.

"Millions of Americans are deeply dissatisfied with their lives and their rulers at all levels. However, these are not yet a revolutionary people, for they still have faith in the institutions of democracy.... As long as people believe that they can elect the right people to lead them, the 'legend of democracy' will unfortunately live on" (Jon George, PE #11/12, Autumn 1991). This "legend of democracy" is certainly the force which governs progressive and leftist politics. It is certainly tempting to believe that somewhere there are good, honest politicians who can both be elected and make major positive changes. Instead it appears that only those who are honest (either in word or deed) about their adherence to the status quo will be considered viable candidates for ruling.

Even if there were somehow the possibility of electing "good" leaders, a problem still exists. This is the problem of the reformist who does not put faith in the individual and the community to solve their own problems. Instead the reformist feels that people cannot manage their own affairs and that an authority is necessary to successfully lead us to better things. "I think it is highly flawed to count on the government to enact social reform towards a more just society since any stateist society is going to be based on class divisions and inequality" (Felix, <u>PE</u> #13, March 1992, 6). The kind of reforms championed by the Left deal with attacking the symptoms of the system rather than dealing with the disease itself. Problems of the homeless and poor are addressed without placing the blame on the whole corrupt system of greed caused by the laws of capitalism. "If anything, it only serves the interest of the ruling class and the state to have thousands of intelligent and concerned individuals devoting their efforts to token reforms which will in no way affect the reigning power structure" (ibid). Thus the Punk anarchist has rejected the way current governments function. It is important now to look at what their possible (or often admittedly impossible) conception of anarchy is and how it differs from what has been criticized.

The first Punk band to take a serious interest in anarchy and its implications was the English band **Crass**. For a detailed history of the

bands origins and adventures, read founder Penny Rimbaud's book Shibboleth. They were as much a community of twelve people as a band, as they also created films, newspapers, and ran a record label. The band formed in 1978 as a reaction against the rising fashionableness and acceptance of Punk. Their business practices are mentioned later as they set a standard others followed regarding merchandising. Only with respect to their views on pacifism have some anarchist Punks renounced them as a major reference point for the Punk anarchist ideal.

"Anarchy is the only form of political thought that does not seek to control the individual through force" (**Crass**, Flipside #23, March 1981). **Crass** condemn both the right and left wing parties as using power to control and coerce people. Having the idea of a state requires that people will subordinate some aspect of their lives to it (in some cases their life itself). "Anarchy is the rejection of that State control and represents a demand by the individual to live a life of personal choice, not one of political manipulation" (ibid). With the rejection of control also comes a certain amount of personal responsibility. For all of the hassles government seems to create, it does involve less personal responsibility and is perhaps easier to live under. "By refusing to be controlled you are taking your own life into your own hands, and that is, rather than the popular idea of anarchy as chaos, the start of personal order.... The state of anarchy is not a chaotic bedlam where everyone is out for themselves" (ibid). Where individuals live with other individuals in trust and with respect.

The question of how anarchists can ensure that living a life of personal choice would be different than present society presents a dilemma. Anarchists could obviously not force people to accept anything, so they expect a kind of necessary learning and internalization process to prevent rampant prejudices and greed. "Respect for other people (and property) cannot simply be demanded, it must be taught. It is our capitalist society with its emphasis on greed and the self, a constant socialization process rein-

83

forced throughout our lives which fosters an attitude of treating people as objects" (anonymous letter, PE #5). In other words, the anarchist, or anyone wanting positive lasting change, must be willing to teach or "socialize" people to their way of thinking on human issues in order to create a successful, free society.

To conceive of any chance of a successful change of ideology without coercion or force, the anarchist must think of humans as being capable of and wanting change. If the case were otherwise, the anarchist would be forcing the very same manner of conditioning he despises. It would be a contradiction for an anarchist to force her beliefs on another, but if people are not greedy, selfish, or hateful by nature then they may be agreeable to the anarchist's ideas. People "are conditioned by society to exploit each other and this is necessary for the system to operate. Surely, if a child was exposed to good pacifistic, humanitarian ideas as opposed to those the child now encounters on a daily basis, it would have a totally different attitude towards society and the world as a whole" (New York band **A.P.P.L.E.**, MRR #48, April 1987). The anarchists must think of all people as equally able to rule themselves or they will become elitist and admit their far reaching goals as impossible. This idea often relies on the presumption that human nature is naturally good evidenced by Kropotkin's observation that all life functions best when practicing mutual aid. Proponents of this thought range from Aristotle to the convincing and prolific works of linguist, anarchist, and all-around good guy, Noam Chomsky. While some anarchists have given up on the masses (a topic that will be discussed), the majority seem to agree that anarchists must become "teachers" to others without, of course, becoming leaders. "Somehow or another, the people must learn about anarchism. Most anarchist propaganda today in effect preaches to the converted" (Jon George, PE).

It is certainly hard for intellectuals and near impossible for the average citizen to take the Punk movement as a serious force for revolution. The false media image of Punk Rockers' sole actions as doing drugs and practicing self-mutilation has done a good job of weakening Punk's political threat. This has not stopped the recent wave of Punks from forming groups to put anarchist Punk's rhetoric for change into action. Throughout the 80's and 90's Anarchist Youth Federations (Minnesota, Tennessee, California and Maryland), Twin Cities Anarchist Federation, Cabbage Collective (Philly), Tools Collective (Boston) , Positive Force D.C. , and others organized gigs, events and benefits with a purpose. Today there are Punk collectives sprouting up and shutting down all over the USA. Perhaps the finest example of this collective spirit has been Positive Force in Washington D.C.

"Positive Force is a group of mostly young people in the D.C. area who work together for change. We organize benefits and free concerts, demonstrations and teach-ins, and also directly work with needy people. We oppose racism, sexism, homophobia, militarism, violence, ageism, economic inequality, and censorship among other things.... Positive Force endorses no political party or leader. We endorse the idea of young people working together for change" (P. F. handout). Positive Force was very active in forming protests against the Gulf War and has raised thousands of dollars for causes such as food banks, the Washington Peace Center, Planned Parenthood, and AIDS centers among others. Although working to benefit these groups may seem stateist or reformist to some of the more radical anarchists, the group has been very successful in raising conscience and building a community. I have personally played (with a band) at one of their organized benefits and was deeply impressed. An entire book could be written on their group, their goals, and their successes. The group's founder (but admittedly not leader), Mark Andersen, is currently writing a book of his philosophy and the history of the Washington D.C. Punk scene.

Again, most of these Punks were influenced by the words and actions of English political Punk bands like

Crass. In particular, **Crass** worked with the Campaign for Nuclear Disarmament (CND) in the early eighties. Steve Ignorant of **Crass** recalls that, "the first time we walked into the CND office at Kings Cross it was just a tiny poky office with two people and all these 60's posters everywhere. We said we'd like to work with you. At that time, Punks started using peace symbols and reading up on war and it really took off. We showed people what their situation really was and that there wasn't anything weak or hippie-ish about peace" (Steve Ignorant, <u>MRR</u> #62, July 1988). In addition to this, **Crass** and other bands started an anarchy center based in London. This center was used as a bookstore, a gig space, and a squat for those who had nowhere else to live. Unfortunately, the center was later closed due to drug abuse and vandalism by those who took "no rules" to mean no responsibility. A similar center, the

Oi Polloi, Enola, Pa, '91

Emma Center in Minneapolis, seems to have avoided these problems.

Before going into the methods used by anarchists to reach their goals and the arguments on pacifism, it must be noted that many anarchists have very limited goals. Many Punk anarchists have been content to stay within their own circle and have rejected the possibility of widespread anarchy. This attitude can be interpreted as a conception of "personal" or "lifestyle" anarchy. Here one would consider himself an anarchist but would resign himself to the fact that other people are not capable of ruling themselves. This idea echoes the epitome of bourgeois culture. The belief that "I'm OK but everyone else is messed up" is not anarchism, but has found a pathetic home in many Punk anarchists' writings.

Personal anarchy is subject to the stateist claim that a government or some kind of law enforcement is necessary to keep the murderers and thieves at bay. Even the most ardent communist or republican will hardly admit needing a government to control herself, saying that it is necessary for the masses. In this way, personal anarchy is elitist, unanarchistic, and counter revolutionary. These people have pretty much given up on the hope for any major changes within society, but still remain active in spreading their views to others. In this way they are still participants in the Punk anarchist community and their views and contributions are still taken into account.

Pacifism has become an increasingly important subject in the anarchist community of late, spurred on by the U.S. invasion of Iraq and the seeking of ways to show resistance. The original anarchist bands favored its practice but now years later, it is being rejected by many of the same people who advocated it. Again, English bands such as **Chumbawamba**, the Scottish **Political Asylum**, and **Crass** were the first to inject this view. "There is no contradiction between anarchy and pacifism. Pacifism is not passivity, to me it represents a deep revulsion at the taking of life... The idea that pacifism is passivity is as naive as the idea of anarchy being chaos" (**Crass**, <u>Flipside</u>). **Crass** were quick to point out that pacifism was not some kind of cowardly response to force. "As a pacifist I stand against organized militarism, believing that the use of power to control people is a violation of human dignity. If I were to find myself in a position where that power threatened to directly violate me, I would stand against it in whatever way was necessary to prevent it. In that situation I do not rule out the possibility of force" (ibid). Pacifists do not desire to be martyrs of any kind, but stress that non-violence is in line with anarchist views. Outside authority is wrong, even when the anarchist is the one in authority. Pacifist Punks have found it hard to spread their views in a community where pacifism is still shackled with its mainstream connotations.

"The majority of people have such set beliefs that any open and determined pacifism is hysterically conceived as enemy infiltration, rather than as an extension of the obvious fact that War is Death is Wrong. Such basic fundamental logic is generally accepted as true but 'unrealistic' in a world of greed and paranoia where patriotism is second nature and survival is taken for granted..." (English band **Subhumans** <u>Rats</u> EP, Bluurg Records, 1983).

Further justification of the pacifist anarchists' views comes from the often debated relationship between ends and means. It will be very hard to complete an anarchist revolution of smashing the state without anarchists resembling the people they are fighting. "I happen to believe that ends and means must be kept consistent. So lying, cheating, killing and similar things are out as far as I'm concerned" (Mike Gunderloy, editor of <u>Factsheet Five</u>, <u>MRR</u> #77, Oct. 1989). For pacifist inclined anarchists, revolution must come about through education. Only by showing, not forcing, people to accept freedom can a true anarchist revolution and society exist. Anarchists who use violence against their enemies often "act from their ego instead of their heart and use violence whenever they feel the need"(Skull, <u>Assault with Intent to Free</u> #9, Fall 1991,

34). Pacifists hold the view that "producing literature and debating an issue will convince people long before a Molotov will"(ibid). The main reason for Punk anarchists to be pacifist lies in the idea of anarchy itself. "With the goals of no government or outside oppression, anarchist violence seems to be more out of tune with the stated objectives than any other political violence" (Todd Masson, editor of IN*CIT, PE #5, 11).

There are other obvious reasons for the Punk anarchist to favor non-violent means. The most obvious is the great difference in numbers and power the Punks and other counterculture freaks have to their respective governments. They certainly cannot topple a government themselves or expect the status quo citizens to support them. Also there is little good that can be done if imprisoned or dead. "Playing with romantic notions of revolutionary violence tends to put people in the ground before their time, or at least in jail... even if most violence is genuine self-defense. What do you hear from well armed, defensive Black Panthers of late?" (ibid). Many Punks have been taken with these romantic notions and committed petty, ineffective crimes or acts in the name of an imaginary revolution. Pacifist Punks urge other anarchists to realize that much has to be done before, if ever, violent action will be necessary or somehow justified in an attempt to create an anarchist society. For now, "the more needless action we produce the more people will write us off as mindless punks who haven't matured" (Skull, AWITF).

There are an equal number of Punks who call themselves anarchists who do not subscribe to pacifism. Some of these are the same people who were originators of the pacifist camp. Members of the English bands **Conflict**, **Chumbawamba**, and Steve Ignorant of **Crass** have all rejected pacifism after repeated attacks by Skinheads and police. Pacifism has become viewed as a naive idea even among many of those who had endorsed it. "Unfortunately the real world isn't based on moral premises. If politics and revolutionary change was just about morals, we'd have won centuries ago!—because in certain times and certain places we need to use violence" (Ramsey Kanaan, **Political Asylum**, <u>MRR</u> #104, Jan. 1992). Even if pacifism has been successfully painted by liberals as an admirable moral code, it may be a tactic used only to our disadvantage. "I believe in the pacifist philosophy, but I can also say I believe in a God but in real life I'd have a hard time proving that one exists! This is real life, and there is very real violence in our society. By not being prepared to deal with it, mentally or physically, is a great risk to take" (Dan, editor of <u>PE</u>, <u>PE</u> #5). Dan and Felix of the <u>PE</u> collective have repeatedly given preparedness information in their magazine. One of the better and more recommended articles can be found in the <u>Making Punk a Threat Again</u> book under the subtitle "Turn Up the Heat" where Felix gives an accurate and much needed firearm primer.

There are no set criteria given to determine when and to what ends violence would be acceptable. One place where conflict has occurred was during the Gulf war protests when pacifism was criticized as being ineffective

Descendents, State College, Pa, '86

and liberal. "That first week of protest in San Francisco was fraught with tension between the pacifist mainstream and those who endorsed a more radical confrontation. We all witnessed 'peace' demonstrators who defended Army recruiting stations, put out fires, and apologized for police arrests; the collective whine of 'No Violence!' still runs through my head" ("The War at Home," <u>MRR</u> #100, Sept. 1991).

That author has rejected pacifism without realizing the spectrum which the view can encompass. He feels that pacifism is defended by a "higher consciousness which manifests itself in a self-righteous Puritanism, forbidding anger and spontaneity. It is founded on a slavish devotion to icons such as classist, stateist, misogynist Gandhi: it creates a colorless mass of wannabe martyrs who fear 'unruly' life energy more than death itself" ("New World Order," <u>MRR</u> #99). While I agree with this condemnation, the author would do well to note that it is not devotion to set rules of protest that can change society but the proper use of tactics to achieve goals. Sometimes violence is necessary, sometimes it is counterproductive.

Admitting that there is violence in our society, and that it is wrong, does not seem to persuade many people away from adding to it. The idea that violent means are the only ones that get results is as dangerous as the "might makes right" argument that anarchists so vehemently oppose. To hold pacifism as an admirable ideal, but useless because of its impracticality, is equivalent to the charges often leveled at anarchy.

It should be said that non-pacifist Punks have not yet caused any great harm to any human beings for any political significance as far as I know. Fights with police had been frequent throughout the early eighties (and are still not rare) but have usually been the result of a canceled concert or party. Punks have not taken part in any violent revolutions or political assassination attempts and are certainly not violence oriented despite what the press may say. Only recently have Punks taken a serious interest in armed struggle. The resurgence of material about the **Red Army Faction**, the **Angry Brigade**, the **Weathermen**, the **Black Panthers**, and other groups of people who chose armed struggle is continually reviewed in fanzines. With the spread of this literature, coupled with the popularity of the Mexican EZLN struggle, more punks are going against the ideology of pacifism. Hopefully those who choose other means of support in worldwide struggle for freedom will be well prepared.

While this violence against authority figures may meet mixed reviews, violence to property has been an active part of both the pacifist and non-pacifist Punks' activities.

Direct action against inanimate objects is used to make statements favoring change. The environmental section details the willingness of some Punks to act in a way that would be considered vandalism or destruction of property. Acts are not often enough publicized to explain their significance, so the general public views these acts as hooliganism. Dutch Punks have bombed Shell gas stations for their ties to South Africa, Punks worldwide have destroyed animal research labs and the property of those who run them, and billboards across several countries have been altered to have political meanings. These acts and many more (against McDonald's, banks, etc.) are all viewed as actions taken against oppressors. It should be mentioned again that pacifists are almost always in agreement with these actions and that their pacifism applies only to living things. During the Gulf War, Punks found that trying to halt the conflict "meant raising the material cost of intervention through property damage and spray paint propaganda; it meant directly impeding military operations by shutting down recruiting stations and blocking weapons shipments at the Concord weapons station: it meant making the necessary connections between war and the elements in our society that propel us along such a violent path" ("New World Order," MRR #100, Sept. 1991).

The fanzine Profane Existence is vocal in their support of the physical destruction of property. Editorials often urge action and the news section applauds such actions. Editor Dan describes his participation in the D.C. war protest: "The first actions took place as we passed the excessively large and expensive looking treasury building. A few tax payers got early refunds when stones were hurled through windows and red paint thrown on walls. Money can buy new windows, but no amount can replace the lives of those lost for the government and its wars" (Dan, MRR #95, April 1991).

Destruction of property is not only seen as a way to make a political statement, but many Punks advocate it as a way to have fun as well. Punks have taken a view similar to that used by groups such as Earth First! regarding direct action. Monkey wrenching and trying to subvert the system are regarded as primary parts of Punk. This action usually does not spread to physical confrontation except when dealing with Skinheads or the police. About the

NOFX, Berkeley, Ca, '92

police, there is perhaps no subject that has been the focus of as many songs, protests, and general antipathy as the police.

"I swear to God, I hate Cops" (Punker in the classic film <u>Decline of Western Civilization</u>) "If I went through every record and tape I own I could probably find about a thousand anti-cop songs by Punk, Hardcore, metal, Oi (Skinhead/Punk music from England), and rap bands. This detestation and hatred of the police are universal across the spectrum of youth sub and counter-cultures.

The police embody everything that is wrong with authority: corrupt, sadistic, racist, sexist, extortionist cowardly scum" (Felix, PE #11/12, 10). There is a definite consensus among Punks that police are scum. They are the pawns and terrorists of state power and certainly have no place in the anarchist's society, where people could police themselves. Punks see police as "a complete waste of tax money, serving no purpose except terrorizing our communities, cities and personal freedoms" (Southern California band **Final Conflict**, Ashes to Ashes LP, Pusmort Records, 1986). Many people claim that police are justified as "just doing their jobs." However if doing their jobs entails harassing and beating those who would dare confront authority, they will receive no kindness from Punks.

This is not to say that every single cop is a racist, sexist bully, but that the "good" ones are few and far between. "Anyone who has been paying attention should know at this point that even on a good day urban police forces are made up of inhuman bastards who revel in their power over others" ("New World Order," MRR #100, Sept. 1991). While some Punks urge passive resistance to the continuous police harassment, others see it as an extreme case where violence is justified. Punks have been involved in countless police confrontations usually resulting in some violence and arrests. It should be noted that European Punks have faced a harder time with their police counterparts than have those in America. European Punks have physically fought back to defend themselves and their squats, and have, on occasion, won. South American Punks on the other hand have been routinely imprisoned and in some cases murdered by police. Even Punks who are vegan pacifists often find themselves using the fascist police force as their exception to the rule of nonviolence.

Anarchist Punks view anarchy as a freedom from authority and rules; a place where people can live their lives without some form of external compulsion. Thus police and even formalized laws would not be necessary. Many Punks have tried to read or promote the anarchist beliefs of the activists Bakunin, Goldman, and Kropotkin, as well as discussing the works of living authors such as Noam Chomsky and Howard Zinn, to show how they relate to the modern Punk movement and its activist goals. Unfortunately, some Punks who consider themselves anarchists have not been interested with the formalities of classical anarchist thought or have been alienated by the apparent "intellectual" aspect of the movement. Discussing the **Crass**-supported anarchy center in England, Steve Ignorant said, "I went to a couple of meetings and the sort of language that was being used was more or less quotes from anarchist writers 100 years ago. I thought that any Punk listening wouldn't understand a single word of it. I got a real sense of this hierarchy, where the people who had read the most Proudhon or whatever were 'top of the table.' To me, that wasn't any different from any other political party meeting—people just sitting around muttering about what dead people had written" (Steve Ignorant, MRR #62, July 1988).

The refusal or inability to study what they were so emphatically endorsing resulted in some having the idea that anarchy is only rioting, fighting with police, and causing chaos. Some Punks were content with expressing rage and destruction as a form of anarchy without its real political connotations. An angry criticism of these folks was written by then MRR columnist, Lookout editor and record label founder Lawrence Livermore:

"Destroy everything now? Yeah, great sentiments for an old-fashioned Punk song, but maybe you ought to bear in mind that there are 5 billion people on this planet that need to be fed, sheltered, and clothed, and if you don't want the government involved in it, you better start figuring out how it is going to get done. Eliminate the basic structures of society (regardless of how badly they work) without first creating alternatives, and you'll produce death and suffering on a scale that will make the Nazi holocaust look like a vegan love feast" (Lawrence Livermore, MRR #76, Sept. 1989).

Others who have this same idea of anarchy as chaos find anarchism to be unacceptable. Their conception that anarchy would be equivalent to the immediate disappearance of police and government, yielding chaos, shows a misunderstanding of anarchism. Anarchists know that there will be no sudden removal of organizations of control, so it is pointless to hypothesize that peoples' reaction to this would be the same as everyday occurrences in an anarchist society. If government forces disappeared today, there would be rioting, crime, murder and destruction on a scale possibly greater than is presently occurring, but that would be chaos, not anarchy. "Anarchy could only be achieved gradually through people changing themselves—and then others by persuasion. You cannot force anarchy on people. Anarchy could only be reality if people controlled themselves—it's about responsibility, being a law unto yourself. Anarchy can only exist when people begin to act responsibly" (Scottish band **Oi Polloi**, MRR #25, May 1985).

The important point to stress is this: anarchy does not simply mean no laws, it means no need for laws. Anarchy requires individuals to behave responsibly. When individuals can live in peace without authorities to compel or punish them, when people have enough courage and sense to speak honestly and equally with each other, then and only then, will anarchy be possible.

Punk anarchists have taken criticism for having an ineffective and fractured community. This is, in part, due to the overwhelming distaste and distrust for any leaders in the movement. "We don't have a leader because we don't want a leader, and this is correct because it is impossible to be a leader without being corrupt" (anonymous letter, MRR #71, March 1989). The very idea of having no leader became so popular that the ones who first said it became the leaders. There came a time when the band **Crass** "would be playing to packed houses of anarchist Punks who knew all our songs, records, and ideas by heart. We were up there saying 'be individuals' while leading a movement full of followers. It's always '**Crass** did this' or '**Crass** said that'..." (Steve Ignorant). The tendency to idolize and copy those with righteous ideas and firm stances has led to a stagnation of free thought and debate within the movement. There are many individuals who are content to do nothing original or act consciously while following very honorable morality and ideals.

While loudly shouting the concepts of individuality, most bands delivered the same message in the same package as the others. It seemed that every anarchist band from 1980-85 had a burned human, starving child, or tortured animal on their record cover in an attempt to shock listeners into action. In an effort to shift the emphasis to unity and away from uniformity, anyone claiming to be a leader has been sharply criticized. Concerning these leaders, "They try to assert themselves as leaders; they put themselves at the focal point of the movement and instead of people evaluating the ideology, they simply watch the actions of these 'loud mouths' and judge the group by the actions of these 'leaders.' These leaders are merely trying to establish their egos: they trust only themselves, completely undermining the actions of the group as a whole" (Skull, <u>AWITF</u>).

The goal of having no consensus spokesperson or leader has been obtained by the anarchist community.

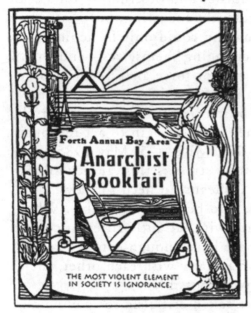

March 27th 1999 10am-6pm

Forth Annual Bay Area
Anarchist Bookfair

THE MOST VIOLENT ELEMENT
IN SOCIETY IS IGNORANCE.

San Francisco County Fair Building
ninth ave & lincoln way in golden gate park
as always, admission is free

However, the result of this has not been the egalitarian co-operative atmosphere that anarchists had wanted to foster. There is now a factionalized and weak movement within which parties squabble more than work together. Disagreements on goals and whether to support sides in stateist conflicts are two of the many factors now dividing the community. The anarchist movement in North America appears to be made up of members with no common direction. "The movement is divided into many splinters with the majority having very closed agendas. Every little Anarchist 'party,' if you will, can not and will not work with anyone or anything else who is not as politically correct" (Dan, PE #2).

The situation appears to be no better in the UK where the most noteworthy events are the Anarchist Bookfairs. "It's estimated that between two and three thousand people turn up at the London ones but getting people to peddle their wares in the same hall is about as close as we can get to getting people together" (Ramsey "the Rod," Kanaan **Political Asylum**). The Punk community in San Francisco has also had positive participation in the now annual Anarchist Bookfair in San Francisco. Each March over 1,000 folks get together to display and shop for anarchist and radical literature. The influence of the Punk movement is evident both in the activists displaying goods and the members of the organizing committee. While little of the featured merchandise is of a specifically Punk nature (and there are no live bands at all) the Punk community is more than amply represented. Punks can play a large role in working to overcome the problems within the anarchist movement. This involves a greater understanding of those they work with and what goals are to be achieved, as well as becoming active and reaching out to other segments of society. Otherwise anarchist Punks will end up frustrated more at each other and their failures than the societies they want to change.

"Anarchists like any other political minority group—whether it be a counter-culture like Punk or an actual political group like a Trotskyist faction—has the tendency to be too inward looking, self-centered and spending more time and energy criticizing others, back-stabbing and on internal squabbling. It's so easy to be a big fish causing big ripples in a little pond instead of struggling to create big ripples in the big, bad world out there! Perhaps if anarchists actually tried firstly, to relate to other people outside their - our ghetto and secondly, address issues that actually affect peoples' lives in the here and now..." (ibid).

The faith that Punks and other activists place in anarchy stems from a belief in the equality and rights of all people. This view of equality is explicitly clear in Punks' visible reaction to sexism, homophobia, racism, and even speciesism. This reaction is to condemn them as being harmful, irrational, and intolerable.

Citizen Fish, Corona, Ca, '96

GENDER ISSUES: SEXISM, FEMINISM AND OPEN HOMOSEXUALITY.

"To me, the idea of the way men treat women is a good symbol for the way the world is run now. It's possessive, it's based on fear and insecurity.... The ideas of nurturing, creating, and accepting to me are feminine virtues. As opposed to the male defects which are owning, destroying, and controlling. The total male attitude and male domination in society has brought us to the point of self-destruction. One of the ways to get out of it is to stop dealing on that level, stop being totally masculine in the way we treat each other" (Canadian band NO MEANS NO, <u>MRR</u> #39, Aug. 1986).

The rejection of sexism by the Punk movement is a continuing fight to educate those who enter the movement with their stereotypical images still intact. Many Punks have taken stands against speciesism, racism, nuclear proliferation, etc., only to contradict themselves by practicing or accepting sexism. While bands often receive strong backlash for using sexist images or lyrics in their records, it is a small but consistent problem. Fanzines and Punk distributors occasionally find themselves having to turn down records or advertisements containing overtly sexist images or lyrics. There is no denying that sexism exists within the Punk community, but it is on a smaller level than in the mainstream, and more importantly, it is discouraged and condemned by many active participants. This is contrary to mainstream society where it is rarely con-

demned or even discussed by anyone other than feminists. Instead of dealing with the negative attitudes similar to those in the mainstream, it is more productive to discuss the views of the active majority of Punks who claim to be anti-sexist.

Women have played an active role in the scene since its beginnings. "In Los Angeles circa 1977, female bass players were almost a requirement, and it seemed that it was often the women who dominated and controlled the Punk scene. This equality of the sexes was just another breakdown of traditional rock and roll stereotypes that the early scene was perpetrating" (Craig Lee, Hardcore California, 20). Sharon Cheslow publishes a zine out of San Francisco entitled Interrobang which gives a fairly comprehensive list of females in early Punk bands. Women in the Punk movement have attempted to step out of their normally limited roles and become primary actors and central makers of change.

"Feminism" has not been designated as a bad word to male Punks. Men's voices have often joined or even out shouted the women's in condemning sexism and coming to the realization of a necessary cooperative atmosphere to best create goals and form ideas. Punks often agree with the simple feminist theory that "the system which enforces male domination harms both women and men. That system is part of the system which perpetuates racism, classism, heterosexism, and all forms of oppression" (PEACE compilation LP, booklet, R Radical Records, 1984, 11). The role of patriarchy in society has been to separate men and women into stereotypes of strong and weak. Women are recognized as the "other" of the two sexes and men are used as the reference point. With this attitude it becomes easy to accept (or for women to relinquish) power and authority over those who are the "other."

The power or strength men have often seems to be derived from their apparent ability to act unemotional, 'hard,' or serious. "Men are socialized to repress emotions, to not cry, to ignore the needs to nurture and cherish the next generation. Emotions, tender feelings, care for the living and those to come are not seen as appropriate concerns..." (ibid). It is quite obvious that men are capable of sensitive thought just as females are guilty of uncaring actions, but the ongoing process of brainwash/conditioning serves to reinforce stereotypes resistant to positive changes. "Being closed about their emotions can put men in a position of power. Opening up about how you feel emotionally can make you vulnerable and open to attack. By keeping their mouths shut, men avoid facing underlying tensions and their part in making them" (English anarchist band **Chumbawamba**, Threat By Example, 29).

As much as men do not want to relinquish that power, many women seek to gain it by adopting stereotypically male characteristics. Clearly Punks' conception of feminism does not involve applauding women who rise (or sink) to men's stereotype of toughness. Women fighting in Desert Storm, female politicians such as Margaret Thatcher, or women who gain authority and prominence in exploitative multinational corporations are not looked upon as inspirations.

Male stereotypes may have created an aggressive, anti-caring approach to problems which has led to the current disorganization and disasters of the planet. Why haven't females been able to correct this? Sometimes they have but usually they are held in check by conditioning of their own. For many reasons, many women do not want to change the way things are. "In high school I remember girls insisting it was really bad to let a guy know how smart you are.... You had to be short, have tits, act lame, not have a strong personality, be agreeable, have no opinions, dress like a whore..." (Cecila, "Exterminate Airheads," MRR #61, June 1988). Stereotypes die hard. Fanzines such as Punk Parents, Hip Mama and The Future Generation, deal with raising children in a stereotype-free environment. Boys are given dolls to play with other than the typical G.I. Joe or aggressive hero figure. Girls are encouraged to play with toy cars and tools as well as dolls.

I am afraid that many Punk parents may be disappointed as their children become conditioned upon entering school (although for obvious reasons many advocate teaching at home if possible) and are forced to conform, if only for a small number of years.

While many fanzines have dealt with feminism alongside the other topics of music and politics, some are now emerging with women's issues as the sole reason for publishing. Riot Grrl fanzine, press, and distribution from the Washington D.C. area is put out by young women for primarily young women. They provide information on both past and present women's movements (much as anarchist fanzines do), women's health care issues, and ideas for positive change stemming from anger and frustration.

"I am here now, and I feel comfortable to go into the world as I please. I should feel comfortable to carry myself as I please, where I please, and when I please.... I will project the strength and anger I feel, ready and armed with rebuttal upon embroilment.... I am not pleased to

photo: Susan Alzner

Indigo Girls & Friends, Chiapas, Mexico

have my sex ridiculed, to be seen as an item, not a free thinking being. I am not 'asking for it' by existing in a space that is rightfully mine, the world" (Ne Tantillo, Riot Grrl, 1991).

Over the last couple of years, the Riot Grrl movement has grown considerably large. The wonderfully produced Angry Women books and widely distributed fanzines such as Bitch, Bust, and Girl Frenzy, have all benefited from and helped fuel youthful female empowerment. Features in large newspapers (N.Y. Times, USA Today, Newsweek) as well as trendy teeny bopper fashion and music magazines have brought attention and spotlight to these ladies, their bands, and their look. While suffering the same problem as any other growing scene: dilution, conformity, shallowness, and 'passing phases,' the fact remains that the female empowerment it promotes is a great thing.

Both women and men in the Punk movement realize the problems women have faced in the world. This has caused attempts to eliminate these problems of mainstream culture from reoccurring within the scene. Fortunately the major feminist movements have already increased women's opinions of self-worth. "Feeling that the balance of power is out of sync has absolutely nothing to do with feeling yourself to be of less worth than a man. I don't know any women in any sphere that really see themselves as inferior beings" (**Chumbawamba**, Threat By Example, 29). From here women have taken it upon themselves to show and educate men of their equality. Feminists who simply wait for men to change their attitudes on their own will have to wait a long time. In an essay on sexism a male brought up an interesting point:

"Feminists, regardless of gender, frequently bemoan that men seem unwilling or unable to change their traditional behavior patterns on their own. Though it may sound heretical, it's worth asking why they should. Because it's right—yes, of course—but most people don't change for purely moral reasons, but because they see changes to

Bikini Kill, SF, Ca. '94

be in their interest. And as long as men can get what they want —or think they want—from women by being aggressive, chauvinistic, insensitive, even violent, then they'll continue to behave that way" (Sign Language compilation EP, Allied Records, 1991).

The response for Punk women is to show that men will not get "their way." The women will "change" themselves. I put "change" in quotes as they can merely act natural and comfortable instead of making the far greater changes involved when striving to fit stereotypes. All of us growing up have seen and experienced the horrible pressure to look or act a certain way. It would seem easier to act natural but given the power of society's conditioning it is not. "Isn't it stupid to insist that men have oppressed us, then insist that men have to change their ideas and FREE us? Girls have to stop acting like bimbos. I know it's hard, it wasn't easy for me..." (Cecila, MRR #61).

Years ago MRR started a section devoted entirely to women's issues and ideas composed of female readers' submissions. This section often brought up the idea that women must take some responsibility for sexism and try to change their own ideas. "What is disturbing is that women are not being called on the shit we do to hold ourselves back, in part, because there is an attitude that women have nothing to do with continuing sexism, because we're victims. Ultimately, I don't see equality in sight until we confront ourselves" (Suzanne Bartchy, MRR #104, Jan. 1992). Even stronger, "it is difficult to oppress half of the world's population if at one time or another that half had not allowed itself to be oppressed" (Lali, ibid). Lali is obviously no student of history or class struggle, but her point that all people must stand up to their oppressor is well taken. Punk women are not very fond of ignorant women who so willingly go along with the mainstream, striving to fit the stereotypes created by society. Women who not only act and dress a certain way for men, but who do it to raise their own self-esteem by being accepted are often blamed along with the men.

Allowing themselves to be oppressed includes actions which are not blatantly negative to women. Even what some consider to be beneficial treatments of womanhood are used to reinforce the oppressed stereotype. "Sexism is placing somebody on a different plane (a pedestal also fits this bill, 'gentlemen').... Do not assume me as a lesser force, and do not worship me as the foreign, ungraspable, incomprehensible, breathing hourglass entity. Both guises set me at a complete disadvantage..." (Claire Slow Drain, MRR #103, Dec. 1991).

An example of this woman worship which has no basis in reality can be found in some modern ecological and social movements (particularly Ecofeminism). I have been confronted in several readings with the idea of a special bond existing between women and nature entitled "nature feminism." The idea is that women are more in touch with nature and therefore are predisposed to be more concerned with the environmental destruction than are men. To take nothing away from the pleasures and pains of childbirth and menstruation, I see no link between it and genuine environmental concerns. Perhaps women often feel a greater bond with their children than the fathers, or are more eager to protect their children in times of danger (results of a patriarchal society where the women is obligated to spend more time with the child than the father is), but as for an extension of this feeling to include unity with "Mother Earth," I am not convinced. Punk women have noticed this as "a turn towards hippy dippy occultism a la the pursuit of 'Women's Mystical Powers.' As far as I can see we don't have any wondrous and mysterious abilities that are directly related to our ability to give birth and menstruation" (Lali, MRR #104). Our goal should be to re-enchant and celebrate our own humanity rather than turn to superficial new age healings.

An issue that has not received great attention is the subject of abortion. This is because the movement is very dominantly pro-choice and has not seen much disagreement. The desire to break the continued oppression of our-

selves and our environment includes protecting the few freedoms the system has allowed, however temporary and small. Rarely does a band speak out against legal abortion and when it has happened they have been severely criticized. Without entering medical or religious arguments surrounding abortion, Punks respect the right of every woman to make her own choice on the matter.

Abortion should not only be legal but, in necessary cases, subsidized. "The anti-choice side wants to stop public funding abortion. They don't want their tax dollars used for something that they don't believe in. Well I didn't want my tax dollars used for the bombs and bullets that killed civilians in Panama. From a cold economic point of view it is cheaper to fund an abortion than to fund the subsequent welfare, food stamps, and housing of an unwanted child" (Beth Roberts, "Pro-Choice for a Reason," Assault With Intent to Free #8, April 1990). In agreement with many other active liberal, radical and human rights movements, Punks view abortion as a freedom or right not to be taken away.

This following quote and final information could have been included in the environmental section but I have chosen to include it here as the ideas are closely related to those of Ecofeminism. Many ideas such as anthropocentrism (a huge word defined as interpreting or regarding the world's value in terms of usefulness for its human inhabitants) and the intrinsic value of nature are covered later.

"Change isn't conducted by 'professional' organizers or experts; it's made by ordinary people showing compassion and cooperation, and standing against racism, sexism, ecological destruction and the terror waged against the earth" (David Spanner, Canadian band **D.O.A.**, <u>Right to Be Wild</u> EP, 1983).

Gerry Hannah (or Gerry Useless) was a founding member of the Vancouver Punk scene in the late seventies and his band the **Subhumans** released several records of inspired, aggressive music with intelligent socio-political lyrics. They played at "several anti-nuclear benefits, a fund-raiser for El Salvadoran guerrillas, a Rock against Reagan show on Ronnie's inauguration, a Rock against Racism benefit for the Pontiac brothers (Michigan prisoners on trial for allegedly killing KKK guards) and an anarchist smash-the-state concert" (ibid). Gerry is a strong believer that actions speak louder than words. In 1983, he and four others (known as the Vancouver Five) were arrested for "bombing a controversial new hydro-electric development opposed by environmentalists: dynamiting the plant that's producing guidance systems for the first strike Cruise missile; and fire bombing three pornography outlets distributing videos containing torture, mutilation, and sexual violence against women" (ibid). While these may seem to be the actions of terrorists to some, heroes to others, knowing why they did them is important. If the ends can justify the means, then what they did may be just or even obligatory.

Gerry had a letter printed in a benefit single put out

Kamala, Cringer, NYC, '91

by the very popular and rockin' Punk band **D.O.A.** in which he shared his views. He justified direct action as the best and perhaps only means available for change. Gerry criticizes those who are politically aware but adopt the attitude that "given time civilization will eventually evolve by itself into some wonderful utopia. Given time by itself, however, civilization will almost certainly develop into an unconquerable police state or will wipe itself out entirely by atomic war or by poisoning the environment" (Gerry Hannah, ibid). He gives a criticism of the anthropocentric view and ties it into sexism.

"Those of us who are men must realize that despite what we may think of ourselves, we continue to be highly oppressive and dominating... we refuse to acknowledge and embrace the so-called feminine aspects of personality such as compassion, sensitivity and tenderness. Instead we deliberately emphasize the negative so-called male tendencies of aggression, competitiveness and arrogance. There appears to be a direct relation between those tendencies and the most serious problems we face today" (ibid).

Gerry sees a direct link between stereotypical male tendencies to dominate nature and the oppression of women. This similarity in treatment and the oppressive results is the essential idea behind Ecofeminism. Until sexism is recognized as a fundamental issue, "all of our efforts toward positive change are hypocritical and sadly lacking" (ibid). There is no justification for favoring or agreeing with just one fight against oppression. They are all fundamentally interconnected. "Only through a complete understanding of our dangerous and dismal situation and the causes behind it, and by adopting a radical outlook towards changing it—including the essential concepts of anarchism, feminism and environmentalism—can we hope to break the chains of oppression that bind us and this planet so completely" (ibid).

While sexism is acknowledged as a rampant and prevalent problem in society, a similar problem often goes unacknowledged. This is the problem of heterosexism, or

Whorehouse of Representatives, Pueblo, Co, '95

homophobia, which many people in society, including women, are not concerned with. Homosexuality has been a visible part of the Punk movement since it first began, and with increasing hostilities occurring against gay people, it is a component that has sparked controversy and become increasingly noticeable.

"**Punk (punk) Slang. noun. 1) An inexperienced or callous youth 2) A young tough 3) A passive homosexual catamite.... What do you know. Punks are fags, too" (G.B. Jones and Bruce LaBruce, Homocore #7, Winter/Spring 1991).**

Punk has been largely composed by people who perceive themselves as misfits or outlaws in one way or another. For some this is because of their physical appearance, dress, or political views. For an increasingly vocal segment of Punk, it is their sexual preference which forces their nonconformity and rejection of mainstream society. Before Punk was a movement with magazines and music, there were "punks." As far back as the fifties, "young boys were being 'turned out' in jail (recruited to serve other prisoners sexual desires) and labeled 'punks'" (ibid). The particular method of dress, attitude, and distaste for authority that characterized these "punks" was used by the mid-seventies Punks in New York and elsewhere. Looking like delinquent hustlers, the first wave of Punk championed a sexual ambiguity and nonconformity that has lasted for years.

There was a book written in 1955 by Donald Cory which discusses the experience of being queer in the United States. While this book is outdated in many respects, The Homosexual in America is very effective in showing the link and attraction between being Punk and being queer. Like Punks, "the homosexual is acutely aware of his lack of acceptance by society and of the difficulties (social, economic, and other) arising there-from. Each moment of chagrin, each instance of humiliation, each act of rejection awakens a rebel spirit which is seldom antagonistic to society, but only to society's offensive and unjust attitudes" (Donald Cory, "From Handicap to Strength," in Man Alone, 420).

More important than accepting one's alienation, the queer must be able to look for the reasons as well as other examples of alienation and oppression outside of his/herself. Cory explains that "the fact of being an untouchable provokes a solidarity with and understanding of other groups of individuals who may be in analogous positions in civilization" (ibid). This understanding is the premise used by Punks in their support of women's rights, civil rights, and the plights of indigenous people among others. If it is true that the young queer will find himself an iconoclast, a skeptic and a rebel to oppression and alienation, then he will in today's world often find himself identified with Punk.

In one passage Cory mentions the open-mindedness of the queer community which could be reproduced in similar fashion with the word "Punk" substituted for "gay." "Among many of my gay friends, no precept, no matter

how dearly held, is allowed to rest unchallenged. No new thought, no matter how absurd it may seem to be, fails to receive its day in court. Whether one discusses politics or medicine, philosophy or literature, no matter how far removed from the world of sex (or music in this case), the homosexual brings a mind that is unusually questioning and skeptical" (ibid).

In today's world many of the gay people fitting Cory's description do not seem to feel any antagonism towards society itself because they see a decline in its unjust attitudes. There seems to have been a token amount of acceptance of the queer lifestyle which has kept many of Cory's "rebel spirits" asleep. There is a gay mainstream full of people whose close mindedness rivals mainstream society's. Having both a straight and gay mainstream provides queer Punks with two status quos to reject.

Many gay Punks feel that the gay movement has been co-opted and is largely meaningless. "The gay 'movement' as it is now is a big farce, and we have nothing nice to say about it..." (G.B. Jones and Bruce LaBruce). Queer Punks do, however, have many bad things to say about it. Contrasting with a view of sexual equality is the veiled misogyny present in the gay culture "which privileges fag (male) culture over dyke (female)" (ibid). It is strange to see a male domination present in the realm of same sex relations, but a visit to gay operated bookstores, bars and businesses in any major city will show that it is the male acting as the primary focus.

The Gay movement has been co-opted, but the Punks do not plan on making the same mistakes. "One way to avoid such co-option is to present a movement that refuses to conform to the standards of sexual decency and moral conduct expected of even the most rebellious of youths, while avoiding the mistakes of the Gay movement: ghettoization, liberal reform, class capitulation. And that's what Homocore, coming out of the pages of a gay softcore pornography fanzine for Punks is all about" (G.B. Jones and Bruce LaBruce).

Both male and female queers are active in putting out fanzines and have made it a point to target the mainstream gays and especially the co-opted male. "Most so-called queers are still duped, still wearing sweaters and getting $40 haircuts. Those guys at the Gay Men's Chorus are still going to drive back home to the suburbs and get richer than any breeder could hope to be" (Larry-Bob, editor, Holy Titclamps #6, Fall 1990). Queer Punks aim to show that "not every homo is an 'assimilationist,' i.e., someone who is gay but wants to be part of mainstream culture, thinks 'equal rights' means women and homos in the army, the right for a shitty job for life, and thinks that freedom of choice means Coke, Pepsi or Seven-Up" (Tom Jennings, editor, Homocore #7).

Homosexual Punks find themselves acting as a double-edged sword, slashing stereotypes in two worlds. They are often loud, proud, and open about their sexuality. Larry-Bob urges Punks to wake up potential queers, who would otherwise be sucked into the mainstream, by being as openly gay as possible. "Every time you kiss your same-sex sweetie in a mall, and some kid sees you, it's another young mind corrupted, another step towards victory. So kiss away!" (Larry-Bob). He suggests that "traveling freak shows" go town to town stopping at every family restaurant possible dressed in bondage gear. "Some preteen fag is going to see a real queer... and realize that there's more to life than interior decoration and get saved" (Larry-Bob).

I stressed earlier that this book was to be on the prevailing attitudes of the active Punk scene. By this I mean the members of the community who do the most to keep it going and determine its course. These are the attitudes of the creators, not necessarily the average consumer. The people who put out records, fanzines, form activist groups, and try to make changes are the creators. Those who participate merely by going to see the bands play music, are the consumers and are for the most part not represented in this book. It is true, though, that consumers can become creators and may bring with them traditional

Tribe 8, Berkeley, Ca, '92

mainstream values. Because of this it is much easier to find Punks who are homophobic than those who are openly racist or sexist. While this moronic ignorance is not a new occurrence, it was not an original part of Punk.

"When Punk made the transition from the classic style to Hardcore, there started a new emphasis, not part of the original idea of Punk, on being 'hard,' and this was identified with being 'macho.' Given the popular image of homosexual activities as 'unmanly,' it is not surprising that homophobia soon became a part—fortunately a very controversial part—of the Punk scene" (Donny the Punk, <u>Homocore</u>). Others feel that the movement of the Punk scene from the city to the suburbs during the early eighties involved adopting suburban values. Whatever the case, the past years have shown a large resurgence of the queer community in the Punk scene and there have been problems.

At a gig in Berkeley, California, I witnessed a very negative reaction by approximately one-third of the crowd to the openly all-lesbian band **Tribe 8**. While the majority of the people were willing to defend the women's right to play, a very vocal and angry amount of men and women were not in approval of the "fuckin' dykes." Admittedly the crowd on this night was drawn by an exceptionally apolitical headlining act (the musically superb **NOFX**), but it does show that the occurrence of such obvious hate and tension has not left the Punk scene completely.

So far I have shown Punk's philosophy of egalitarian principles as it relates to human beings. The ideas are based on rejections of racism, classism, sexism and hetero-sexism. In the upcoming pages I will attempt to show that these principles apply quite frequently to the non-human world of animals and nature as well.

(above) Poison Idea, Boston, Ma, '90
(left) Chumbawamba, Berkeley, Ca, '92

NO MASTER'S VOICE

RESI$T

GO VEGETARIAN!

Logging Bridges Destroyed

THE A.L.F. IS WATCHING AND THERE'S NO PLACE TO HIDE!

DEEP ECOLOGY, NOT DEEP SHIT!

Direct Action Speaks Louder Than Words

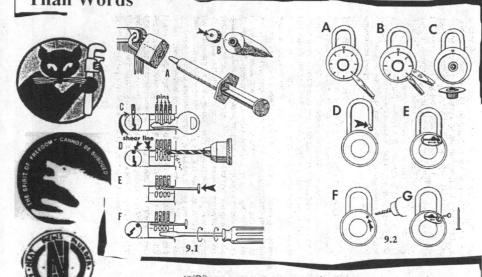

I DON'T EAT ANIMALS AND THEY DON'T EAT ME!

¡FURDER!

FROM PROTEST TO RESISTANCE

ENVIRONMENTALISM AND ECOLOGICAL CONCERNS: THE IDEAS AND TECHNIQUES OF EARTH FIRST, ALF AND OTHERS HAVE FOUND A COMFORTABLE HOME IN THE PUNK SCENE.

"And if the animals could talk, if the planets, the trees, the rivers, the mountains and the oceans could cry out their protests, they too would demand an end to the destruction that greedy men and women have caused. Self-preservation is our greatest instinct, yet we have been so misled, mis-informed, mis-educated, tricked and fooled by the profiteers, that even caring mothers and fathers teach their children self-destruction and destruction of the planet unconsciously every day from birth. It would seem that as world culture grows more intelligent and sophisticated, that civilization would come closer to providing for the needs of all people and solving social problems, but instead, those who are in power have chosen the exact opposite direction, inflicting more hunger, more exploitation, more racism, more pollution, and a system of military dictatorship and dominance over all the world populations" (PEACE compilation LP, booklet, R Radical Records, 1984).

Clearly, the Punk ethic of individualism must take a back seat when thinking of global preservation terms. In the case of environmental philosophies, practices, and protests, the emphasis is on the whole, not the part. From various texts and recorded material it can be shown that the whole is made to include not only mankind, but animals and nature (meaning wilderness, rivers, etc.) as well. Here we will deal more with the non-animal environment.

Punks reject the "Cowboy Ethics" that have governed environmental policies and actions in America for over two hundred years. This attitude has led to disastrous effects to both the environment and the ideas relating to its improvement and recovery. The ideas and actions which we have come to romantically identify with Native Americans (whether rightfully or not) are much more of an influencing factor on the Punk philosophy. "Just as we have the technology and resources available to destroy the world more than 100 times over, we have everything we need to provide for all the needs and rights of every living being on the planet, and respect our mother earth as the kind provider of life that she is.... When the life of each living being and the laws of nature are respected and when mother earth is respected as the giver of life to all, then there will be peace" (ibid).

There seems to be no large glorification of primitive, pre-industrial societies or anti-technological biases in the Punks' view. There is little talk of dropping out of the system or living in agricultural communes. The movement is basically an urban/suburban one which does not idealize rural life. However, the acknowledgment of respect and commitment to a 'healthy mother earth' can be easily seen as a common thread linking Punk philosophy to a pre-industrial, pre-colonized perspective.

While there will always be different opinions coming from under the Punk banner, the most evident environmental philosophy closely resembles something called Deep Ecology. This philosophy has been around for most of human time in one place or another and is readily seen in the writings of Henry David Thoreau and others. The term was coined in 1971 by the Norwegian philosopher Arne Naess and later popularized in Devall and Sessions' 1973 book <u>Deep Ecology</u>. One article written in <u>MRR</u> by Joel Hippycore details the similarities of the Punk environmental philosophy to the ideas of Deep Ecology. "What is needed to effectively combat humans' past destructiveness is a comprehensive philosophy that does not put humans against Nature, but instead places humans in their proper ecological niche" (Joel Hippycore, <u>MRR</u> #77, Oct. 1989).

The most important aspect of a radical philosophy is the shedding of current misconceptions, regardless of how popular or widely held they may be. One of the largest and hardest to change may be the accepted anthropocentric or human centered way of viewing the world. It has been argued (successfully in many cases) that Biblical traditions of God giving man dominion over the plants and animals of earth are largely responsible for this view.

Whether caused by the Biblical interpretation or Natural Law hierarchies recorded by Aristotle and Thomas

7 Seconds, Camp Hill, Pa, '84

Aquinas, anthropocentrism is an underlying precept in nearly every philosophy and political theory ever written. It is a belief that humans are separate and superior to Nature. "With a view such as this, thoughts of humans living in harmony with Nature cannot be entertained" (ibid). Like Devall and Sessions, the Punk community is attempting to foster a biocentric philosophy in response to environmental problems. This view contains the realization that everything in nature is inter-connected and has equal intrinsic worth. Nature is respected and cared for, not dominated. This should not be confused with a conservationist view.

"Conservation is drenched in anthropocentrism and is therefore an unacceptable ecological perspective. The goal of conservation is to manage and control nature as part of the human economy, not live in harmony with it.... Trees become cash crops and wilderness preserves are for attracting tourists' dollars: Nature is not viewed to have any value in and of itself.... Humans have a vital need for wilderness to help us mature, but what is more important wilderness has a right to live without human interference simply because it is—it has a value independent of its usefulness to humans" (ibid).

Many practitioners of deep ecology have taken it to be a new religion. Several rituals and celebrated dates have been observed for the reasons of reaching inner feelings or becoming more in touch with nature. As can be expected Punks reject the religious component of the philosophy. "...celebrating the solstices and equinoxes is as superfluous as celebrating Christian holidays. Individually they may be of great impact, but ecologically they are completely disposable." (ibid) Whether Punks subscribe strictly to a form of deep ecology or create their own variation of biocentrism or holism is debatable. What is obvious, however, is the consistent stress on the deep ecological belief in the need for direct action.

"There are two types of direct action, inward direct action involves developing a deeper maturity and losing one's anthropocentric view. Outward direct action can take the form of monkey wrenching, protest, civil disobedience or the planting of a tree. There is no sharp break between inward and outward direct action and both are guided by one unyielding principle: nonviolence. Direct action is the realization that we cannot turn away and ignore the earth's problems, we must do something. Everything is inter-connected, by protecting the rain forest we are protecting ourselves, and so by taking direct action one expresses the utmost love for the planet and its inhabitants... Action is the goal, and action itself must be the truth, its own defense, and its own purpose" (ibid).

While Punks may argue over the best means of a non-violent action, the idea of employing direct action is not debated. Much of the environmental action is linked to the northwestern United States and in particular Northern California.

Scared Of Chaka, New Orleans, La, '95

"What is happening in Northern California is similar to what has been going on in Latin America and other U.S. colonies for the past century. The main difference is that they're not shooting at us, at least not yet. But for all intents and purposes, we are a third world economy. The majority of the people are poor enough that they're happy to take any job that pays a living wage, even if it means destroying their environment and leaving a wasteland for their children" (Lawrence Livermore, <u>MRR</u> #84, March 1990).

Livermore and other fanzine writers made appeals in the summer of 1990 for Punks to join with the Earth First! activist group to act against the deforestation in California. "I don't mean just writing to your congressman, or signing a petition, or attending a demonstration, or writing magazine articles, though all those things are important. I'm talking about putting your hearts and souls and your bodies on the line to stop this madness before it destroys us all" (ibid). In <u>Profane Existence</u> magazine Earth

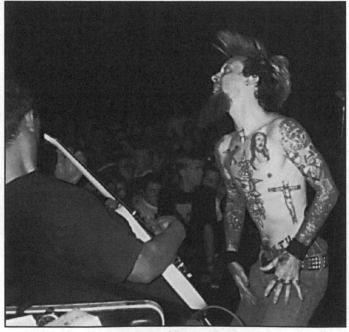

Avail, Indiana, '96

First! placed an ad which included "We are putting out a call to Freedom Riders for the forest to come to Northern California this summer and defend the Redwoods. We hope to maintain permanent encampments and waves of actions all summer long" (Profane Existence #5, Aug. 1990, 37). Many Punks are members and supporters of Earth First!, Greenpeace, Animal Liberation Front, People for the Ethical Treatment of Animals, and other groups. Books such as Ernest Callenbach's Ecotopia and Ecodefence: A Field Guide to Monkey Wrenching by Dave Foreman and Bill Hayward first came to my attention through suggested reading lists enclosed with records.

Profane Existence's news section includes articles that applaud, glorify and encourage action against environmental threats. Commenting on the deliberate destruction of a bridge used by a British Colombian logging firm to access the trees: "A company stooge was quoted as saying, 'All I know is I'm going to have to tell a lot of people that they're out of work.' Not to mention you and your corporate money grabbers stand to lose hundreds of thousands of dollars in profits. Once again, a hearty boo fucking hoo" (PE #11/12, Autumn '91, 4).

Beefeater,
Harrisburg, '85

In a recent issue of PE a long and well researched editorial was written about the problems caused by construction of golf courses in America. Animal killing pesticides, trapping, water waste and unnecessary and wasteful land development were reasons to encourage some form of direct action.

"Each golf course green costs about $18,000 to build and many more thousands to maintain, so if you're going for maximum damage that's where you want to start. One simple way to thoroughly fuck up a green is to pour liquid chlorine or pool acid on it (available at any pool supply store). Gasoline will also work. This will make the expensive turf turn yellow and die, costing loads to repair. Try to do this when the lawn is dry if possible. Experiment with other toxic liquids as well; sabotage can be fun and educational!" (ibid, 46).

While written in a humorous vein, the article shows the Punks' willingness for action and allowance of violence against property.

The Punks feel the reasons for the continued destruction of the earth can often be found in economical greed. The major consideration of polluters is staying in business and increasing profits. The government does not like to interfere with profit making enterprises, especially when jobs are involved. In many cases such as in Northern Wisconsin, "The state government is doing its best to bring in the mining companies. The politicians in power want to remain in power by creating new jobs and increasing tax revenue" (Tom Coyne, MRR #100, Sept. 1991). From mining to lumber to the new craze of stadium building (particularly here in SF where two unnecessary new ones are going up) politicians are able to cover the topic of irreversible ecological devastation with the false promise of employment to the area's residents. Those of us who live in impoverished neighborhoods chosen to be the recipient of environmental racism/capitalism can see how the promise of desperately needed job opportunities blinds us to permanent destructive developments. It seems apparent that ecological costs are not being considered and that it is leading to disaster. The scale which measures costs in dollar increments does not accurately weigh ecological costs into the equation.

Small farms in particular, which tend to make more of an effort of organic or sustainable farming, are having an increasingly hard time making financial successes.

"But what is such a farmer to do when a large company buys up the adjacent 5,000 acres, spikes the soil with potent fertilizers, plows out all the wind breaks and protective contours, and sinks deep wells that suck out ground water twice as fast as it can be replenished? In the long run such techniques will lead to disaster, but in the meantime they will produce large yields that drive prices down, and if the small farmer doesn't adopt similar techniques to keep up with the competition, he's out of business" (Lawrence Livermore, editor of Lookout #31, Summer 1988).

New California legislation being pushed by corporate food giants is aimed at the labeling of pesticide soaked and genetically altered foods as organic. This legislation, if passed, will put the true organic/sustainable farmer under pressure to adopt the same quick yield techniques of the corporate farms which exploit both the land and the health of farm workers and their families. This may be the final success giant farms need to finally put the small farmer out to pasture once and for all.

What can we do? Even those who do not approve of outward direct action are able to use the power of action to protest environmental problems involving the producers (whether they be farms or other producers).

"Whether we like it or not, we live in a consumer society. At the same time that the bands and fanzines of the Punk community speak out against multinationals, we do have to spend money in the system for our needs. Therefore it follows that we try to avoid the dehumanizing trash that the corporations spew out at us as much as possible. With persistence, this can be done easily in several areas" (Assault with Intent to Free #9, Fall 1991). One of the best ways to refuse and resist a destructive capitalist system is to vote economically, spending dough where you feel it has the least harmful effect. Many fanzines today include a section for publicizing products to be boycotted. These boycotts can be called for issues such as useless animal testing, unfair labor practices or immoral profit investment. Various other zines have listed helpful hints on reducing, recycling, and reusing products. Nowhere is the philosophy of preserving and improving the environment more evident than in discourse on food and diet.

"Omnivorous man would appear to have adapted well to many strange and bizarre foodstuffs that have emerged out of the lab and the factory, but perhaps it is still too early to tell. Life expectancies are greater than at any time in recorded history, but so is the occurrence of diet related illnesses like cancer and heart disease" (Livermore). A rational look at the wasted resources, health issues, and the acceptance of a deeper or more humane ecology has caused a growing number of Punks to become vegetarians.

*(counter clock wise) Jasper, Phil,
Trotsky: Citizen Fish*

"The factory is churning out all processed pack-aged and neat/ An obscure butchered substance and the label reads 'Meat'/ Hidden behind false names such as Pork, Ham, Veal and Beef/ An eyes an eye, a life's a life the now forgot belief" (Conflict, It's Time to See Who's Who LP, Mortarhate Records, 1986).

Vegetarianism and animal rights are two subjects which were first popularized by the European Punk community. English bands, particularly those with anarchist messages, often included in their records information and images on the horrors of animal use and abuse. Politically minded Punks have viewed our treatment of animals as another of the many existing forms of oppression. "Punk is about freedom for people and animals too. Punk is against discrimination in the forms of sexism and racism and also speciesism. 'Man' has no right to abuse and inflict pain and misery on other living creatures who have as much right to freedom as we" (Scottish Punk band **Oi Polloi**, <u>MRR</u> #25, May 1985).

The concept of animal rights is a frequently mentioned and debated aspect of modern Punk. Most Punks seem to follow Pete Singer's view on the issue (he is often quoted and listed as a suggested reading), holding the suffering of the creatures to be the fundamental argument against their use and the reason for legitimate rights recognition. There is little evidence of the holistic environmental idea that allows for (and in some cases obliges) the killing of animals, even in debatable cases of overpopulation. Punks do not contemplate the possible ecological disasters caused by mass vegetarianism while a large majority of people (especially Americans) still consume animal products. The animal overpopulation problems suggested by holistic philosophers such as J. Baird Caldicott seem to be disguised attempts to hold up the status quo. Humans have progressed far enough scientifically to exist without the excessively cruel treatment of our fellow animals. To progress that far morally is not as easy a step, as it involves a shuffling of priorities and the rise of inconveniences. These difficulties are however nowhere as great as the ones currently faced by animals and undeniably going to be faced by humans in the resource depleted future. Humans are no longer in a Darwinian state of nature where people must kill and use animals to survive. The persistence of carnivorous activity strengthens not only the smug notion of human superiority but the legitimized use of violence and oppression.

"Human beings are responsible for destroying rain forests, polluting the air and water, and basically ruining our own environment so let's stop using the excuse of 'superior intelligence' as an excuse to dominate and destroy all other life forms on the Earth" (The ALF is Watching LP, booklet, No Master's Voice Records, 1990, 5). Some Punks do not deal with criteria of superiority but ascribe rights, much as Tom Regan does, on the basis of sentience. Even if it could be proven that humans are superior, "we have no right to use those whom we deem inferior to eat or experiment on, no matter if it is a great benefit to us or not. For in the grand scale of things, we have no more right to life and liberty than any other thing" (ibid). This idea is drawn from the biocentric/deep ecological view discussed earlier.

Even Punks who do not acknowledge the concept of animal rights and hold strong anthropocentric views have been known to change their diet for purely environmental reasons. The wasteful and rapid destruction of both

Swiz, Harrisburg, Pa, '87

land and water resources involved in raising livestock cannot be ignored. Others have converted simply for health reasons, this is common amongst Straight Edge Punks. Tips on converting to a vegetarian diet have been presented in countless fanzines including <u>Flipside</u>, <u>MRR</u>, <u>Assault with Intent to Free</u>, <u>Profane Existence</u>, <u>Hippycore</u>, and many European fanzines such as <u>OX</u> (Germany) and Australian ones (<u>Fight Back</u>...) as well. The editors of <u>Hippycore</u> have even written an entire book of vegan recipes (including beer) entitled <u>Soy Not Oi</u>. Another Punk-related vegan cookbook, <u>Bark and Grass</u> was assembled in the D.C. area.

While it was the European Punks who promoted vegetarianism, many North Americans are now taking it a step further by promoting veganism. Vegans generally do not consume any animal products including any dairy or eggs. Some see veganism as a way to "abstain 100% from a form of cruelty that I perceive in the world around me" (Canadian band **Engage**, <u>MRR</u> #100, Sept. 1991). While vegetarianism is a step in the right direction, many vegan Punks view it as not enough. The Canadian band **Propagandhi** rips out pro-vegan lyrics such as "Meat is still murder/Dairy is still rape..." with a tunefulness not heard before in political Punk. In their song "White Blood" the band **Naturecore** writes, "The blind use of dairy products is overlooked by even 'vegetarians!'/ There are many alternatives to milk, cheese and eggs./ To support this deadly routine is a crime in itself" (**Naturecore**, <u>The ALF is Watching</u> LP, booklet, 1).

Vegans argue that humans can live healthy lives with a diet based around soy products, grains, and other plant life. They are right. The main reason vegetarians do not convert to a vegan diet is the inconvenience, or else it does not satisfy their taste buds. "There is no other truthful explanation. No moral justification. Veganism is cheaper, healthier, and even tastes better (once you've been off of the animal products long enough to break the artificial man-made craving you once had for them)" (ibid, 4). I can vouch for a vegan diet being healthy and plentiful; however I do not feel the need for a person following a non-vegan diet to offer moral justification for their choice. While an important choice, diet is not the most important thing to focus your lifestyle on. More importantly is the way we treat each other as human beings in our quest for a better existence.

The idea that our treatment of animals influences our treatment of each other was hinted at earlier. "This violence which surrounds us all the time and takes so many forms is right here in our food. You have certain things in your character which yearn to satisfy aggressive impulses by chewing, chewing on the blood and flesh of other creatures" (**A State of Mind**, Animal/Humyn Exploitation EP, Mind Matter records, 1987). Feeding and encouraging this aggressiveness acts as a possible link between human and animal oppression.

"It's the same barbaric mentality which allows thousands of men to be slaughtered on the battlefield of war, just to benefit the filthy rich, that causes millions of animals to be murdered in the name of science, or for food, clothing etc., that whether it be animal or human exploitation the cause is the same—an attitude that one has the right, for their own personal desire, not only to have others serve, but also die for them" (ALF is Watching LP, booklet, 2). The Punk philosophy tends to believe that the exploitation of animals is another step towards allowing the exploitation of people.

The concept of animal rights goes beyond vegetarianism/veganism to encompass a strong anti-vivisectionist view. This point is evident in the large amount of benefit records and tapes that have been put out to raise money for the Animal Liberation Front (ALF). Although it has been shown time and time again that vivisection is largely a waste of time and money (and lives), proving that it somehow benefits mankind would not be enough to make it acceptable.

Punks have turned to the ALF partly due to their direct action techniques, partly because mainstream

NOFX, Berkeley, Ca, '92

animal rights groups often give the cold shoulder to Punks who do not adhere to their conformist protest tactics, but mostly because the ALF succeeds at its mission. The ALF is an animal rights group that uses direct action to free lab and farm animals. Formed in England, the group has carried out actions in Canada, the U.S., and other European nations. "We believe in taking direct action in rescuing animals from vivisection laboratories, factory farms and other cruel establishments, and also causing damage to property belonging to animal abusers and animal abuse establishments—to prevent animal suffering and cause financial loss, and eventual financial ruin to those who persecute defenseless creatures" (ALF Supporters Group handout). "Other cruel establishments" have included fur

BGK, Dillsburg, Pa, '85

dealers and butcher shops. At these action sites messages are often left behind (in a note or spray painted on the wall) to explain the reasons behind the action. This is done to show society that the activists are not merely purposeless vandals or terrorists and to hopefully prevent backlash from the rest of the community.

The support of action over lobbying attempts has a strong tradition in the Punk movement. While Punks may not have the connections or resources to work with lawmakers, they often will try to change things themselves as directly as possible. Fanzines have printed interviews with ALF activists who tell where, when, and how to cause problems for their enemies. Rhetoric, as the following quote demonstrates, has inspired many Punks to not only act on their own but to form their own groups (PAL - Punks for Animal Liberation in CA...) and educate others in the quest for animal liberation.

"The ALF are a great inspiration, hopefully a great enough one causing others to come out of their shells of fear and act! We can do it! Together we can become hit and run guerrillas in a war the state has chosen to create. A physical threat, not backed by mindless violence, but one driven by knowledge and love. The love of all life, humyn and non-humyn. And through these acts of love we will destroy their towers of greed and institutions of death. We will create a world of peace, in harmony with the earth and each other" (**A State of Mind**).

Vegetarianism and animal rights have become staples of the concerned Punk's political philosophy. However, the largest growing number of converts to vegetarianism have been the recent wave of Straight Edge Punks who swear off meat mainly due to the artificially created desire for it, and are often not receptive to other ideas of Punk's radical thought. Straight Edge Punks are not as concerned about changing society as they are about ending personal obsessions. For this reason they do not drink alcohol or smoke, and in some cases refuse caffeine or sugar. Their attitude towards eating meat is similar to that of drinking alcohol, it's unnecessary, unhealthy, and harmful.

Avail, Corona, Ca, '98

Government Issue, Enola, Pa, '86

STRAIGHT EDGE: A MOVEMENT THAT WENT FROM BEING A MINOR THREAT TO A CONSERVATIVE, CONFORMIST NO THREAT.

"...I'm a person just like you but I've got better things to do/ then sit around and smoke dope cuz I know that I can cope/ I laugh at the thought of eating ludes I laugh at the thought of sniffing glue/ always want to be in touch, never want to use a crutch/ I've got Straight Edge!.." (Minor Threat, "Straight Edge," Minor Threat EP, Dischord Records, 1981).

In 1981 the Washington D.C. Hardcore Punk band **Minor Threat** released a song which begat a movement within the Punk scene. With the intent of spreading a positive and personal message, the Straight Edge movement (named after the song of the same title) quickly spread to Boston and much of the East Coast. The message was simple: you do not have to drink alcohol, smoke, or indulge in any mind altering drugs to have a good time. Straight Edge caught on fast with suburban teens who were feeling the peer pressure to engage in alcohol, etc., and were rejecting it. Bands such as the mega-positive unity driven **Seven Seconds** in Nevada, hardcore units **SSD** and **DYS** in Boston and the **Necros** in Michigan were some of the first to adopt the ideas being used by the thriving D.C. scene. In fact, **Minor Threat** and the Dischord label were eager to offer their assistance in the releasing and distributing of these bands' recorded output.

Local Punk scenes quickly became more youth oriented and took their shows away from the clubs and bars, which depended upon alcohol sales, to rented out fire halls

and V.F.W. posts. Straight Edge brought bands and their lyrics down to a more personal level for the kids facing peer pressure and gave many the support to reject drugs. As a teenager, I was seriously blown away by the full throttle live shows of **DYS**, **Verbal Assault**, and would drive hours to go ballistic at **7 Seconds** gigs all over the East Coast. What these bands offered was a hardcore alternative to both straight society and the English "drunk punk" we couldn't identify with. All of the first wave of hardcore Straight Edge bands and many of the second wave acts put on high energy live shows outside of the bar scenes that tended to dominate the boring rock'n'roll world. The new intensity and conviction of this music brought back to life a Punk scene that had begun to stagnate with political sloganeering and "party time" attitudes. **Minor Threat**'s lyricist and singer Ian MacKaye's goal of "controlling things and not letting them control you" (**Minor Threat**, <u>Flipside</u>

Speak 714, Bayview SF, '97

#34, Aug. 1982) was echoed throughout the American Punk community, eventually growing in places as far away as California in 1984-8 (**Uniform Choice, Insted**...) and Europe in 1988-present.

The audiences drawn to Punk by the media of the mid-80's gave little thought to Straight Edge and as a result it slowly became a weaker force in the national scene. Most of the originators had either gone on to different kinds of music (slow plodding hard rock or alternative pop ala **U2**) or began to drink, smoke,... as they grew out of their teens. The once influential Straight Edge scene gave way to a violent and ignorant media inspired Punk population. Commenting on the scene in 1985, MacKaye said, "I don't feel there's that much focus. It's like everyone is just here to party.... I don't need to go to any Punk Rock show for that. I want to go out and do something with my mind, and do something with some sort of direction.... I want purpose. I want my life to count for me, for some-

Ex-Straight Edger

thing. I'm not just here to have a good time" (Ian MacKaye, Hard Times #7, June 1985).

MacKaye has indeed progressed musically and philosophically since 1981, and his bands have remained inspirations for thousands of people. For an incredibly detailed account of the Washington D.C. Punk scene, its history and the lives of its characters, (MacKaye being the main focus along with **Bad Brains** and others), check out Mark Anderson's hopefully soon to be published volume Dance of Days: D.C. Punk 1975-95. The book gives a blow by blow history of the D.C. Straight Edge scene in an incredibly favorable light.

MacKaye has remained both politically and socially active with his band, **Fugazi**, and although he does not drink, smoke, or even eat meat (later added by many as an integral part of Straight Edge), he is unwilling to preach Straight Edge or even call himself a part of it anymore. This unwillingness to label himself as Straight Edge is, in part, because of the way his message has been twisted and adopted by a new wave of young people. In response to the ignorance of the mid-80's, the Straight Edge reaction was a movement of close minded, intolerant youths who condemned Punk and many of its ideas.

"A lot of bands list us as an influence, but they're so intense about shoving all this down people's throats that I want to tell them that I think they've really missed the point" (**Seven Seconds**, MRR #72, May 1989). If Straight Edge set out to make kids think for themselves and be themselves, today's Straight Edge movement has indeed missed the point. The late eighties and current times have witnessed an extremely large growth in the popularity of Straight Edge Hardcore. The new bands and fans have become increasingly reactionary, conformist, and macho in the last few years. The bands copy the musical styles of the earlier bands as well as the artwork for records, typical hair styles (as normal and acceptable as possible), and clothing (athletic wear). As a result of conveying such Puritan messages in such a forceful way, Straight Edge has become a sea of middle class young white men with little interest in rebellion or radical politics.

Straight Edge Punks look more like high school athletic stars than the traditional stereotyped Punk. Many Straight Edgers have rejected Punk because of its negative image and now have their own subculture within the counterculture. What started out as a way to improve Punk and escape peer pressure has turned into a scene of self-righteousness and sheep mentality.

Often Straight Edgers will aim criticism at Punks who are not straight. About Punks who drink beer, "You pump your money into corporations that kill people, pollute the earth, do animal testing, make sexist ads, ruin families, cause drunk driving, alcoholism, and are responsible for child abuse, rape, and murder because people were under the influence, etc. How can you be all politically correct without being straight? It doesn't make sense" (Anonymous letter, <u>MRR</u> #103, Dec. 1991). It certainly doesn't make much sense for an anti-sexist to support beer companies with sexist advertising (many Punks are now

Circle of Shit, Lancaster, Pa, '85

147

taking an interest in home-brewing because of this and the obvious reason that large brewers make shit beer), or knowingly support the other things (if one really believes that it is the alcohol companies and their products that cause these disasters and not the people involved).

The Straight Edger who wrote the letter, however, shows that although one may have to be straight to be "politically correct," being straight is not a guarantee of correctness. "You sleazy and gluttonous bastards, with the way you live your sleazy lives, you deserve to have AIDS, it's your fault! ...I am not prejudice against homosexuals as people, but I despise the act of homosexuality. Just the same way I hate cigarette smoking, but not the smoker. I am not homophobic" (ibid). Straight Edge has become (much like Skinheads) a place for homophobic, mainstream macho attitudes to be injected into the Punk scene. While it is impossible and illogical to condemn those who choose not to drink, it is necessary to condemn those who choose not to think.

It may seem unfair to categorize and label Straight Edge in such a negative vein. The intentions and original actions of the movement were certainly well meaning and for a while, successful. Today, however, instead of efforts to improve Punk Rock, they have created a different scene that now needs improving. There has been a most visible rift in cities such as Boston and New York where Straight Edge has clearly become anti-Punk. Even in California, home of the party, Xedge shows are held in large money making established venues where Punk bands have a much harder time getting shows or selling their records. Perhaps the greatest rift and most absurd difference has been caused by Straight Edge youths discovering religion and "turning Krishna."

The largest of the second wave of Straight Edge bands was New York's **Youth of Today**. Their singer, Ray Cappo, went from being a short haired jock to a Hare Krishna devotee. Ray says that "the only way to go beyond Straight Edge is to take Krishna consciousness" (Ray

Cappo, <u>MRR</u> #79, Dec. 1989). Partly due to his religious influence, the Straight Edge principles of no intoxicants and no illicit sex were expanded to further stress no meat eating.

Young kids had blindly emulated **Youth of Today** and when Ray turned Krishna, many followed. It is not rare to see Krishna Straight Edge bands and records. The Krishnas could not have asked for a better spokesperson to recruit new followers. This trend has contrasted sharply with Punks' rejection of organized religion (especially cults) as being oppressive, escapist, anti-individualistic, and just plain dumb.

Still, there are many Straight Edgers who will label themselves as such and consider themselves Punks as well. These people are continuing the original purpose and while often longing for the "good old days" are still a constructive and welcome part of the Punk movement. As with Skinheads there exists a spectrum of participants including radical Straight Edge Punks, gays, women...

In the first edition of this book I was reluctant to mention the tiny "hardline" scene. Back then it was limited to a few groups with few releases and very small followings. I did so only to point out the idiocy of their movement and its intentions. Since then, it has grown exponentially with the shit metal band **Earth Crisis** at its axis. While I applaud the band for their animal rights and Earth First! style endorsement of political action, the overtly reactionary puritan bullshit they espouse is only good for a mocking laugh at best. This band and the many they have influenced were preceded by the SoCal band **Vegan Reich** (try not to laugh at the name). The band **Vegan Reich** along with their record label No Master's Voice had become fairly popular within the scene while espousing very controversial views. Among those views were veganism, an end to animal experimentation, and eventually a peaceful anarchist society. Also present were views which were blatantly sexist, homophobic, and totalitarian.

Concerning women, "I consider women to be completely equal to men, both in the struggle and in relation-ships, etc. However, I do not think we are the same" (**Vegan Reich** <u>PE</u> #3, April 1990). A fine enough statement unless the differences he perceives serve to justify his sexist opinions. Since he does not consider women to be the same as men, he puts down feminists "who seek to negate pre-set natural roles and destroy the family structure" (ibid). Obviously the support of these roles does not jive with Punk's view of equality. It is blatantly sexist and could easily justify a domination of women. Ecofeminists and others would notice the obvious contradiction between freeing nature from exploitation while confining women to their "pre-set natural roles."

Concerning homosexuality, "from a natural and moral outlook on life, homosexuality can be seen as nothing but a deviation from nature. And like all other deviations from nature, which have brought our world to the dreadful state it is in today, it must be spoken out against and combated" (ibid). A statement of such ignorance requires no need to read into the meaning of it.

And finally and most anti-Punk, "We do believe in anarchism as an ultimate goal, but realize that at this point in time too many humans in the world are weak and unable to resist hedonism. The first step would be a dictatorship by Vegans who would help speed up the natural evolution process by re-educating those who can be, and weeding out those beyond help. After this has occurred and the human race is drastically reduced in population..." (ibid). Dictatorship, mass murder, and fascism are not very Punk or tolerated by most Straight Edgers. The fact that there is any audience for such ridiculous thoughts says something bad about the Straight Edge scene.

It is important to realize that Straight Edge is a good concept with a good purpose. The idea behind Straight Edge was not to take freedoms away from anyone. Straight Edge was a reaction to the constant peer pressure to do what makes some uncomfortable. The idea has kept many halls receptive to Punk concerts that would have otherwise closed due to drug induced violence and vandalism.

Indeed the chief cause of Punk clubs and squats being shut down is often related to drugs and alcohol. The current trend for Straight Edge has been to separate themselves from Punk and create some very critical differences. If this trend continues and a bigger rift occurs, the two may become completely incompatible. For a detailed account of the Straight Edge world, check out the book <u>All Ages</u>. Published by Straight Edge record label Revelation Records, it's all you need to know about the thriving (at least until you're 21) culture.

Subhuman Dick and Fanatics

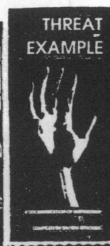

THREAT - EXAMPLE

WORDS AND ARTWORK BY

EPICENTER ZONE
an all-volunteer run store/community center

EPICENTER ZONE 475 VALENCIA 2nd fl SAN FRANCISCO, CA 94103 (415)431-2725

Punk/Hardcore/Garage Industrial/Grunge/Noise/Thrash

Volunteers always welcomed
Meetings 1st & 3rd Sun of month 6:30PM

we buy, sell, trade
new & used records/tapes/CD
fucking unbelievably cheap

Mon-Fri 3-8PM, Sat noon-7PM, Sun 1-7PM, closed Mon-Tues

BLACKLIST MAILORDER

RADICAL RECORDS

ALL YOU WANT IS MUSIC?

Too Bad.

WIMMYN'S RIGHTS FESTIVAL

ABC NO RIO
156 RIVINGTON

NEW YORK CITY'S ONLY NON PROFIT, VOLUNTEER RUN, ALL AGES SINCE

SATURDAY / 3PM / $5

MAY 4 — NO SHOW
MAY 11 — PSYCHO (MA) THE DEVIATORS DOG (TIRED) (NY) OPPOSITION
MAY 18 — VICTIMS FAMILY (CA) STARVATION ARMY (LON) SKITZ (NJ) (?) MERU
MAY 25 — YUPPICIDE ONE (SMALL) DOG (MA) CRISIS MEDIUM JAM HOUSE (CT)
JUNE 1 — URGENT FURY NOTATIONS (N.J.) SMITH (?) JON JORE DEAD SANCTUARY
JUNE 8 — INTELLIGENT CHILDREN (MA) SUGARSHOCK (NJ) MAXIMUM ROACH (CT)

BOOKING / SHOW INFO WILL 718-672-2307 / 718-291-1911 (PM)

NO RACIST, SEXIST OR HOMOPHOBIC BANDS WILL BE BOOKED!

BY-PRODUCT MAILORDER • no answers • no answers • no answers • #10

AN ALL-AGES MEMBERSHIP CLUB LOCATED IN BERKELEY
SHOW INFO: (415)525-9926
BOOKING: (415)524-8180

KNOWLEDGE

IMAGINATION

ZINES
TAPES
RECORDS
BUTTONS

CONSCIENCE

TERRORIZING THE NEIGHBORHOOD:

Noam Chomsky

THE HARD LINE
AND OTHER STORIES

SPERRY

COEXIST: BP 77-75623 PARIS CEDEX 13-FRANCE

MORDAM RECORDS
PO Box 420988
San Francisco, CA 94142

KEEP WARM • BURN OUT THE RICH

DANGER ! TECHNOLOGY AT WORK

RENOUNCE ALLEGIANCE.
STAY ANGRY.
FUCK AMERICA.

DESTROY!

CREATE CHAOS.

DIY

"The driving ethic behind most sincere Punk efforts is DIY—Do It Yourself. We don't need to rely on rich business men to organize our fun for their profit—we can do it ourselves for no profit. We Punks can organize gigs, organize and attend demos, put out records, publish books and fanzines, set-up mail-order distributions for our products, run record stores, distribute literature, encourage boycotts, and participate in political activities. We do all of these things and we do them well. Can any other youth-based counterculture of the 80's and 90's claim so much?" (Joel PE #11/12, Autumn 1991, 10).

The best examples of business practices within the Punk movement are seen by looking at its musical side. Punk Rock has differed from standard Rock and Roll not only in sound, lyrical content and performance styles, but also in the way bands do their business and interact with the audiences. There has been little acceptance of "rock stars" within the movement and bands wanting large amounts of money to play or for their records are continually criticized and exposed. This goes back to the beginning of Punk when there were few people in the movement and the idea of making a great deal of money from the music was a ridiculous pipe dream. Band members were no different from the audience members both in beliefs and often skill as well. The Punk Rock groups "urged other people to form their own groups—it tried to break down the traditional star/audience boundaries. Anyone could be the "star" or no one could be!" (David, <u>Pop and Politics Do Mix!</u>, April 1991, 13). All one needs are the equipment and the desire to form a Punk band.

Punk bands have traditionally helped each other out by getting shows in other towns, setting up tours, putting out records, etc. There have been few cases of competition outside of the number of bands who regularly "sell-out" to gain larger audiences and profit. Punk bands tend to play only with each other as they have similar ideas about cooperation and lack the competitive attitudes that are so prevalent in the music business. The Dutch Punk band **The Ex** gives an indication of one of their typical gigs, where there is "no hassle about being the 'main' or 'support' act as each band is equally important. Helping each other out when it comes to lending equipment, and a fair division of the money. This all sounds so very easy and normal, but in the rock culture such an attitude seems to be rather unusual. That's why we hate rock stars, especially the 'alternative' ones" (**The Ex**, <u>Threat By Example</u>, 72).

These alternative rock stars are bands or members of bands who at one time had a message similar to Punk or were Punks themselves. Their crime is usually jumping from a smaller, independent label to a larger corporate record label (CBS, EMI, Epic, etc.) to gain more money or fans. Many of these bands think that the end (reaching a larger audience) justifies the means (becoming part of a major label). This idea is often rejected and condemned.

"I've too often heard rebel bands excuse their participation with big business labels by saying 'we'll get across to more people.' I'd be interested to discover exactly what they'll get across and to whom. Turning rebellion into cash so dilutes the content of what they're saying that I no longer think they're saying anything. At least the stars who peddle shit and shit alone are up front about being in it for the money. When being in it for the money is being dressed up as politics, I feel like I'm being cheated on two levels instead of just plain patronized by crass music." (**Chumbawamba**, <u>Threat By Example</u>, 31).

Can a band really keep a radical, uncompromising political stance whilst working for a major label whose job it is to sell records to a mass audience? Even if a political band can ignore its major label colleagues (no doubt mindless pop music or sexist rock), and the fact that most labels invest in other businesses (EMI Records was at the time of Britain's Punk explosion owned by a leading arms manufacturer), there will still be a problem with censorship of any threatening message that would harm record sales.

"The committed artist is in an insidious position in capitalist society unless his/her commitment is to the system and to his/her success within it. Above all, the radical songwriter and singer who genuinely wants to use the transmission channels provided by the commercial music industry has more problems than most. The music industry wants to make money using radical rhetoric, but when rad-

Toxic Ranch, Tucson, Az, '95

icalism oversteps the mark and becomes politically committed, a distinct uneasiness rumbles through EMI, the BBC, and IPC"(Dave Harker as quoted in <u>Pop and Politics Do Mix!</u>, 11).

Many of the original Punk bands of the mid-70's were later signed and exploited by major labels. It took the

Los Crudos, Pueblo, Co, '95

first wave of British anarchists and California Punks to realize that they could do records on their own. This way they could set their own prices, write their own lyrics and play the music that they felt was important with no threat of compromise. "This new wave of anarchist politicized Punk Rock held the major labels and the whole established music business in contempt. They refused to play the game. These bands stood firm to the original Punk ideals of independence and anti-establishment" (ibid, 13).

It is important to recognize that while in the past Punk did not have a very large audience in North America, the success of several English Punk bands (most notably the **Sex Pistols** and **The Clash**) left major labels scrambling to sign as many "rebellious" Punk bands as possible to capitalize on the Punk trend. Many English bands including **Crass** and **Conflict** were offered large contracts to sign to EMI. These bands refused to compromise. "Their music and political beliefs meant more to them than that. They weren't in the business of marketing their rebellion for mass consumption" (ibid, 15). One exception is the arty anarchist Punk turned radical Disco band **Chumbawamba**, who has recently signed to a major for new releases and possibly the rights to their past catalog. Only time will tell if they choose to keep a radical edge or fall into the void of monotonous dance music.

By working for a major label and giving them the right to market a band's songs, art work, lyrics, and image for them, a band places commercial success over creativity and messages. Since the publication of this book in '92, **Chumbawamba** have gone on to sign with EMI, censor their lyrical package and allow the label to do absolutely positively everything to place their commercial success over their political message. For all of the people who say **Chumba** "sold out," you are completely right. **Chumba** gave up on being a Punk band years back and have contradicted many, many things they have said relating to the politics of independent music. What **Chumba** have gained by selling out (even if for a flash in the pan) is an opportunity to live comfortably as musicians and donate huge sums of money into the hands of important radical activities. Watered down message and contradictions aside, they may be doing more than all of their critics combined to benefit anarchist politics. Hopefully **Chumba** will continue to support and be a part of the radical political scene even if under consistent attack by their fellow revolutionists. For the puritans of the class war movement and those who would like to read a healthy criticism of the band and their often wavering politics, check out the pamphlet <u>Educating Who About What</u>. It's a rather harsh reality check containing a well deserved attack aimed at the band and their sheepish followers.

Until recently few American bands have been the target of major labels, and as a result there are literally thousands of independent labels operating. In addition to the underground DIY labels, many of these "independent" labels are actually fronts for the majors and are aimed at producing "alternative" music for today's college and mod-

Propagandhi and crew '96

ern rock radio stations. By
bank rolling "independent"
labels and urging them to
sign larger Punk and alternative bands, the majors
attempt to capitalize on
both the independent
minded bands and listen-
ers. Aside from these
"independents," many
bands have made a new
jump to full on major
labels. This comes with all
of the promotion and plas-
tic production that goes
with mainstream acts.

Green Day, **Bad
Religion**, **Rancid**,
Jawbreaker, various
"grunge" bands, the

SNFU, Enola, Pa, '86

Offspring, **Helmet**, and others have made the fast and
powerful riffs of Punk music available to the masses
through radio airplay and large arena type concerts. Their
sounds can already be heard influencing newer pop and
mainstream bands who have no knowledge or interest in
the mentioned bands' Punk roots or histories. While this
trend makes for more entertaining radio listening when
stranded without a tape deck, I do not feel that the people
consuming this "new" music (which is not new, as all of
these bands have multiple underground releases and long
histories) have any clue to the radical nature of these
bands or their roots.

Still, there are bands who continue to stick with underground, truly independent methods of recording,
releasing and touring. The most shining example of retain-
ing independence and ideals while selling more and more
records is the Washington D.C. band **Fugazi**.

"**Fugazi** is an assault on traditional rock'n'roll in the best Punk tradition. The Punk revolution erupted out of disgust over the pathetic state of rock'n'roll. Put simply, rock has become Big Business, corporate capitalism in action, rife with consumerism to a frightening degree. The irony of left-wing, anti-corporate performers like **Billy Bragg**, **The Clash**, **Midnight Oil** or others criticizing the corporate domination of our world while themselves working with mega-corporations to produce, distribute and sell their records is not lost on **Fugazi**. They have turned down numerous major label offers, vowing never to hook themselves to the corporate greed train. Instead of the club circuit they have played in church basements, community centers, high schools and even Lorton Prison. None of their U.S. shows have ever cost more than $6 and the shows have always been open to all ages—unheard of in a rock world where ticket prices for a band of **Fugazi's** popularity are routinely $15 or more and where virtually all bands play in bars closed to all under the age of 18-21" (Mark Andersen, Washington Peace Letter, Nov. 1991, 8).

Fugazi were certainly not the first band to do-it-themselves. Managers for Punk bands are few and far between and until recently contracts for records and shows were virtually non-existent. Records are sold for cheaper than average prices and are available straight from the bands themselves or the few stores that will carry them. The influential anarchist band **Crass** were perhaps the first to sell their records cheaply and they even put profits towards helping other bands record their music. "**Crass** ran themselves on a self-sufficient basis organizing their own tours, records and distribution. Their sole concern was to make enough money to live, not to have top 40 hits or play a large stadium" (Pop and Politics Do Mix!, 14).

It should be noted that almost no Punk bands are able to live off of their earnings and the idea of making large sums of money off Punk (without exploiting it) is not a very popular or feasible idea. This does of course present problems for anyone who wants to have a successful record store or club that is based solely on Punk music. The small audiences and the low concert and record prices maintained by Punks are not suitable for sustaining a project with many expenses. Because of this most Punk record stores and clubs are short lived in even the highest Punk populated areas.

Smilin' Phil

"The beautiful comparison to Punk Rock is the big business world. You don't have rock'n'roll fans running their music business, you've got businessmen running it and making big giant bucks. Punk is not regulated by commercial agents, managers, producers, and shareholders and is not pushed around by big business. If people go into Punk to make millions, they eventually have to get out of Punk Rock because they certainly aren't going to make that kind of money here. You see thousands of bands, labels, zines, and promoters who come from the people who enjoy the music, the philosophies and the ideas. World Punk is truly grass roots" (Chris BCT - owner of a tape and record label, <u>Threat By Example</u>, 44).

This is not to say that it is impossible to have a successful Punk business, but it is near impossible. With help from <u>MRR</u>, the Epicenter record store in San Francisco has been operating for over seven years. Epicenter is an extremely large store with perhaps the largest selection of Punk-only records and fanzines in the world. It is an extremely impressive store and functions as a community center for Punks and sometimes the outside community as well. "Epicenter is a not-for-profit and entirely volunteer run space where the emphasis is not simply placed upon Punk music as a product to be bought

Sell-outs

Youth Brigade, Baltimore, '86

and sold but upon Punk as a realm" (<u>MRR</u> #101, Oct. 1991). Records at the store are comparatively inexpensive and the large amount of volunteers allow the store to be open every day. Epicenter has served as an important example of putting Punks' words and ideas into action and reality. There are similar spaces opening and closing all over the country at such a rate that it is impossible to keep track of their status.

Clubs run by Punks have been much more frequent although equally hard to maintain. Also started by <u>MRR</u> is the Berkeley based Gilman Street clubhouse. The club has been open for twelve years now and has had all-age shows every weekend. A unique aspect of the club is its member-ship policy. While membership policies are usually thought

Cringer, NYC, '91

of as exclusive or discriminatory, theirs is not. "Anyone can join for a mere $2 and a commitment to participate in a violence-free, vandalism-free environment. Because of the danger of getting busted, no alcohol will be allowed inside either" (<u>MRR</u> #42, Nov. 1986).

　　While other clubs (i.e., bars) in the area feature Punk bands, Gilman is the only regular one that is all-ages and non-profit. All shows are six dollars or less and bands from around the country (and world) are invited to play. The volunteers running the hall have changed many times over, and many feel that it is turning into "just another club." While it does seem to have lost much of its original excitement, Gilman Street remains one of the only Punk volunteer run centers around, and that by itself is an accomplishment. Other clubs in England (the 1 in 12), New York City (ABC No Rio), Dallas (Slipped Disk), and Harrisburg (the Core) have attempted to achieve Gilman's success on smaller scales with varying degrees of achievement.

Much more common than Punks who run their own clubs are Punks that organize and set-up shows at rented halls and churches. The problem in doing this is that hall owners are often reluctant to rent out a second time after witnessing the outrageous appearances of some fans and the loud music related to Punk shows. Many people just do not want Punks renting their halls because of the media image they are familiar with.

One group that has had success using rented churches and schools is the Washington D.C. based Positive Force. Like Gilman, Positive Force does only all age, drug-free, inexpensive concerts. These occur only once a month and are often packed out attendance wise. Unlike Punk clubs and many other promoters, Positive Force does only benefit concerts for political causes and provides the audience with a literature table and often political speakers between bands. Positive Force has organized benefits "for causes opposing racism, sexism, militarism, drug abuse, homophobia, animal experimentation and economic inequality among other things" (Mark Andersen, Positive Force hand out, 1990).

Perhaps more important than the causes chosen to be benefitted are the way the benefits are conducted. "Positive Force does not wish to be part of the rock'n'roll club/fashion/image/fame game. All of our shows are all ages. Punk was about the kids reclaiming rock'n'roll for themselves, for the grass roots, making the rock aristocrats and the corporate money-mongers irrelevant. Positive Force is still committed to that vision" (ibid). It should be noted here that Europe has maintained a steady number of Punk squats which also function as clubs where bands play. These are usually run illegally, but serve as a prime example for the ability of Punks to organize themselves and their concerts without outside help.

The ethos of Punk business has been "do-it-yourself." This is an extension of the anarchistic principles requiring responsibility and cooperation in order to build a more productive, creative, and enjoyable future.

"The idea of not relying on the prevailing outside forces in society to create for us to consume is a truly subversive development in our age of ever-increasing centralization, technocratic rationalization, and behavioral manipulation. Even as you read this, thousands of frustrated, creative individuals in all parts of the globe are communicating directly with one another via channels they themselves have helped to set up. A tenacious and growing underground network exists for the dissemination of ideas, information, and self-produced materials, one which transcends the artificial boundaries that unnecessarily divide independent minded people. Whether this network eventually consumes itself in a frenzy of anti-authoritarian elements to challenge national and international power elites, or simply remains as it is, festering and, by its very existence, cutting through the facade of 'consensus' that everywhere holds us in servitude, is anybody's guess. I prefer to leave predictions to the 'experts' who are trying to figure out what we're all about" (Jeff Bale, Loud 3D, edited by Gary Roberts, Rob Kulakofsky, and Mike Arrendondo, IN3D Press, San Francisco, 1984, 83).

BIBLIOGRAPHY

A State of Mind. Animal/Humyn Exploitation EP. San Francisco: Mind Matter Records, 1987.

Animal Liberation Front Supporters Group. Handout. London: 1988.

The ALF is Watching compilation LP. Laguna Beach, CA.: No Master's Voice Records, 1990.

Andersen, Mark. "**Fugazi** - Rhythm of Change". Washington Peace Letter. November, 1991: 1.

Various homemade handouts given out at shows in Washington D.C.: 1985–1991.

Aronson, Elliot. The Social Animal. San Francisco: Freeman and Co., 1972.

Assault with Intent to Free fanzine. Various quotes. P.O. Box 8722, Minneapolis MN 55408: Issues #8 and #9, 1989–91.

Conflict. It's Time to See Who's Who LP. London: Mortarhate Records, 1986.

David (no last name available). Pop and Politics Do Mix! fanzine. Lancashire, England: April, 1991.

DOA. Right to be Wild EP. Vancouver, Canada: 1983.

Final Conflict. Ashes to Ashes LP. Los Angeles: Pusmort Records, 1986.

Flipside fanzine. Various quotes. P.O. Box 363, Whittier CA 90608: Issues #23, 34, 45, and 48, 1981–86.

Hard Times fanzine. Interview with Ian MacKaye. Trenton, NJ: Issue #7, June, 1985.

Hardcore California. Edited by Peter Belsito and Bob Davis. San Francisco: Last Gasp Publishing, 1984.

Henry, Tricia. Break All Rules! Ann Arbor, MI: University Microfilms, 1989.

DoughBoys, Washington D.C., '88

Holy Titclamps fanzine. Various quotes. P.O. Box
591275, San Francisco CA. 94140: Issues #6 and 7,
1990–91.

Homocore fanzine. Various quotes. P.O. Box 77731,
San Francisco 94107: Issue #7, Feb. 1991.

Lookout fanzine. Various quotes. P.O. Box 1000,
Laytonville, CA: Issue #31, Summer 1988.

Loud 3D. Edited by Mike Arrendondo, Rob
Kulakofsky, and Gary Roberts. San Francisco:IN3D Press,
1984.

Man Alone. Edited by Eric and Mary Josephson. New
York: Dell Publishing, 1962.

Maximum RockNRoll fanzine. Various quotes. P.O.
Box 460760 San Francisco CA 94146: Issues #18, 19, 22, 25,
39, 42, 48, 49, 53, 61, 62, 71, 72, 76–79, 84, 95, 98–100,
103, and 104, 1983–92.

Minor Threat. Minor Threat EP. Washington. D.C.:
Dischord Records, 3819 Beecher Street, NW Washington
D.C. 20007. 1981.

PEACE international compilation LP. San Francisco: R
Radical Records. 1984.

Profane Existence fanzine. Various quotes. P.O. Box
8722, Minneapolis 55408: Issues #1–9 and 11–13, 1989–92.

Sign Language compilation EP. San Francisco: Allied
Records, 1991.

Subhumans. Rats EP. London: Bluurg Records, 1983.

Tantillo, Ne. "Comfortable and Free". Riot Grrl
fanzine. P.O. Box 7453, Arlington, VA: Issue #5, Summer
1991.

Threat By Example. Edited by Martin Sprouse. San Francisco:
Pressure Drop Press, 1989.

PENNY RIMBAUD (A.K.A. J J RATTER)
Shibboleth: My Revolting Life
$10.95/£6.95 • pb • 1 873176 40 6 • 352 pp
The extraordinary autobiography of Jeremy John Ratter, a.k.a. Penny Rimbaud, founder, lyricist and drummer of CRASS, a band unique in the history of rock'n'roll. Crass took the idealism of punk seriously. From 1977 to their breakup in 1984, Crass almost single-handedly breathed life back into the then moribund peace and anarchist movements. They birthed a huge underground network of do-it-yourself activism, fanzines, record labels, activist action groups and concert halls. While remaining on their own independent record label, and steadfastly refusing any interviews with the major press, they managed to sell literally millions of records. In this book, Penny takes us from his strict lower-middle class childhood and his experiences in art school to the CRASS years, the hippies and Free Festivals.

PENNY RIMBAUD (A.K.A. J J RATTER)
The Diamond Signature: A Novel in Four Books & The Death of Imagination: A Drama for Four Readers
$10.95/£7.95 • pb • 1 873176 55 4 • 256pp
This book is what Penny Rimbaud considers his most important work. The Diamond Signature formed the basis for the band CRASS, who literally revolu-tionized both punk rock and politics in a blistering seven year career that found them reviled by the mainstream but revered by hundreds of thousands in the underground they helped to create.

GEE VAUCHER
Crass Art and Other Pre-Postmodernist Monsters
$24.95/£18.95 • pb • 1 873176 10 4 • 112pp
A stunning collection of collage and art from the graphic maestro behind the anar-chist punk band CRASS. Vaucher's work—from the innovative wraparound record sleeves to the posters and spray-paint stencils—is seminal to the "protest art" of the '80s, imitated by the underground and ripped-off by the mainstream. This book offers the first opportunity to view Vaucher's work from its art-school origins to the present day. Offering 112 pages of full-color plates and a text detailing the historical context of the work, it promises to be a release of major importance to art lovers, politicos and, perhaps most importantly, to the thousands of people to whom Crass were, and still are, a major inspiration.

NOAM CHOMSKY
Propaganda and Control of the Public Mind
$20.00/£15.00 • double CD • 1 873176 68 6
"The war against working people should be understood to be a real war. It's not a new war. It's an old war. Furthermore it's a perfectly conscious war everywhere, but specifically in the US...which happens to have a highly class-conscious business class.....And they have long seen themselves as fighting a bitter class war, except they don't want anybody else to know about it."—Noam Chomsky, from the CD.
The latest in the audio series bringing Chomsky's finest lectures to compact disc, and perhaps his most important to date. An introduction to, and synthesis of, his key thinking on the media, propaganda and its pivotal role in the relentless class struggle being waged daily.

OTHER NOAM CHOMSKY ON CD:

Class War: The Attack On Working People
$12.98/£11.99 • single CD • 1 873176 27 9

Free Market Fantasies: Capitalism In The Real World
$13.98/£11.99 • single CD • 1 873176 79 1

Prospects for Democracy
$14.98/£10.99 • single CD • 1 873176 38 4

The Clinton Vision: Old Wine, New Bottles
$12.98/£9.99 • single CD • 1 873176 92 9

NOAM CHOMSKY/CHUMBAWAMBA
For A Free Humanity: For Anarchy
$18.00 • double CD • 1 873176 74 0
Disc One: the Noam Chomsky lecture 'Capital Rules'
Disc Two: Chumbawamba's "Showbusiness!," recorded live in 94, as a benefit for Anti-Fascist Action. (*not available through AKUK)

MUMIA ABU-JAMAL
All Things Censored, Vol. 1
$12.98/£12.00 • single CD • 1 902593 06 5
Here are the radio commentaries, the last of them recorded just two days before
Pennsylvania prison authorities instituted a media ban to further silence the most
famous death row prisoner in the US. To hear his voice is to understand why the
state is going to such extremes to silence him. Included are an NPR commentary
by the late great William Kunstler, also banned by NPR, and brief statements or
readings of Mumia's work by Alice Walker, Dorothy Allison, Robert Meeropol,
Howard Zinn, Sister Helen Prejean, and Judi Bari.

HOWARD ZINN
A People's History of the United States: a lecture at Reed College
$20.00/£15.00 • double CD • 1 873176 95 3
Here Zinn explains with great humor and passion how his teaching, his history
and his activism are parts of the same project. The recovery of the stories of social
movements—labor, civil rights, feminists, anti-war—are usually left out or grossly
distorted in mainstream history writing. The efforts of Zinn and others to recover
and pass on those stories offers to their students, to their readers and to us, mod-
els, ideas, inspirations for how and why we might go about challenging and changing the structures of power.

THE EX
1936: The Spanish Revolution
$24.95/£13.95 • hardcover book with double 3" CD • 1 873176-01-5
Within the deluxe hardcover, you'll find previously unpublished photographs from
the CNT (Spanish anarchist trade union) archives, documenting the heroic revolutionary struggle from 1936-1939, with text in English and Spanish. Includes
two 3" CD singles with two Spanish anarchist songs and two original composi-
tions, all performed by The Ex—everyone's favorite anarchist-art-agitators.

VARIOUS ARTISTS
Return of the Read Menace
$10.00/£9.00 • single CD • no ISBN
A benefit CD for AK Press featuring new/unreleased tracks by Propagandhi,
Screeching Weasel, NOFX, Avail, Submission Hold, Randy, Wat Tyler, Quixote,
Chumbawamba, Rhythm Activism, Weakerthans, J Church, Robb Johnson, Ron
Hawkins, Pitchshifter, Consolidated and the Marginal Prophets. All presented in a
full-color John Yates masterpiece of revolutionary art.

JELLO BIAFRA
Burning Down the Magic Kingdom
$17.95/£15.00 • pb • 1 902593 01 4
The first collection of the extraordinary written work of Jello Biafra includes such classics as Die for Oil Sucker, Grow More Pot, Message from our Sponsor, Mild Kingdom, Why I'm Glad the Space Shuttle Blew Up, Wake Up and Smell the Noise, If Voting Changed Anything, Murder of Mumia Abu-Jamal and dozens more. Full of illustrations by Winston Smith.
Jello Biafra, artist, activist, and anti-pundit was a candidate for mayor of San Francisco in 1979; his candidacy forced a run-off election for Diane Feinstein and resulted in a new law forbidding people named Jello from running for mayor again. He and his mates in Dead Kennedys were the first musicians dragged into court for the content of a record, a traumatic event which sealed his life-long relationship with Tipper Gore.

JELLO BIAFRA SPOKEN WORD:

If Evolution Is Outlawed, Only Outlaws Will Evolve
$19.98/$14.98/£15.00/£10.00 • 3 x CD/3 x CS
1 902593 04 9 CD/1 902593 05 7 CS
His latest release. Includes "Depends on the Drug," "Murder of Mumia Abu-Jamal," "The New Soviet Union," "Talk on Censorship" and much more.

Beyond The Valley Of The Gift Police
$19.98/$14.98/£15.00/£10.00 • 3 x CD/3 x CS
1 902593 11 1 (CD)/1 902593 12 X (CS)

High Priest Of Harmful Matter
$16.98/$11.98/£12.00/£9.00 • 2 x CD/2 x CS
1 902593 13 8 (CD) /1 902593 14 6 (cs)

I Blow Minds For A Living
$16.98/$11.98/£12.00/£9.00 • 2 x CD/2 x CS
1 902593 15 4 (cd)/1 902593 16 2 (cs)

No More Cocoons
$16.98/$11.98/£12.00/£9.00 • 2 x CD/2 x CS
1 902593 17 0 (cd)/ 1 902593 18 9 (cs)

FRIENDS OF AK PRESS

In the last 12 months, AK Press published around 12 new titles. In the next 12 months we should be able to publish roughly the same. Our regular readers will have noticed that some books announced in last year's catalog are still not published. Money is tight, and once the stock market crashes, the pittance we circulate among ourselves will shrink even further. We need your help to make and keep these crucial materials available. However, not only are we financially constrained as to what (and how much) we can publish, we already have a huge backlog of excellent material we would like to publish sooner, rather than later.

Projects currently being worked on include: first-hand accounts from Kronstadt survivors; an English translation of Alexandre Skirda's acclaimed biography of Makhno, The Black Cossack; a lively history of the George Jackson Brigade; the autobiography of perennial revolutionaries, the Thaelmans; the first translation in English of the complete works of Bakunin; a collection of prison stories from ex-Angry Brigader John Barker; an account of US prison revolts of the '60s and '70s and the crackdown on activist prisoners since; further translations of the work of Vaneigem; and much, much more.

The Friends of AK Press is a way in which you can directly help us to realize these and many more such projects, much faster. In the US, Friends pay a minimum (of course, we have no objection to larger sums) of $15 per month, for a minimum three month period (a $45 total for three months, $15 each additional month), by check, money order or credit card. In the UK, Friends can have their bank automatically send £10 each month into the AKUK publishing fund—contact AKUK to sign up. In return, Friends receive (for the duration of their membership), automatically, as they appear, one FREE copy of EVERY new AK Press title. Secondly, they are also entitled to a 10% discount on EVERYTHING featured in the AK Press Distribution catalog, on ANY and EVERY order. Groups or individuals can also sponsor a whole book. Please contact us for details.

CONTACT AK

To place an order, become a Friend of AK, or request a catalog, you can write or call AK Press in the US or in the UK at:

P.O. Box 40682, San Francisco, CA 94140-0682
ph: (415) 864-0892 • fax: (415) 864-0893
email: akpress@akpress.org • on-line catalog: www.akpress.org

P.O. Box 12766, Edinburgh, Scotland EH8 9YE
ph: (0131) 555-5165 • fax: (0131) 555-5215
email: ak@akedin.demon.co.uk